A POCKET GUIDE

ISTANBUL

Written by Barnaby Rogerson and Rose Baring
Peace and Quiet section by Paul Sterry

First published 1993 as *Essential Istanbul*
Reprinted February 1995
Revised second edition 1996
Reprinted March 1997
Reprinted January 1998
Reprinted as *Pocket Guide Istanbul* 2000

Published by AA Publishing, a trading name of Automobile Association Developments Limited, whose registered office is Norfolk House, Priestley Road, Basingstoke, Hampshire, RG24 9NY. Registered number 1878835.

Distributed in the United Kingdom by AA Publishing, Norfolk House, Priestley Road, Basingstoke, Hampshire, RG24 9NY.

A CIP catalogue record for this book is available from the British Library.

ISBN 0 7495 2472 3

Colour separation: BTB Colour Reproduction Ltd., Whitchurch, Hampshire

Printed by: Printers S.R.L., Trento, Italy

Front cover picture: Ayasofya mosque (AA Photo Library – Paul Kenward)

Contents

This book employs a simple rating system to help choose which places to visit:

✓ 'top ten'

◆◆◆ do not miss
◆◆ see if you can
◆ worth seeing if you have time

Maps and Plans

Introduction and Background

INTRODUCTION

There is a particular buzz in Istanbul these days. People from all over the world crowd around the makeshift market stalls in Beyazit Square like the pigeons that flock here to take seed from the charitable. Here an Uzbek family from beyond the Caucasus congregates round their colourful silk-suited matriarch. There a gaggle of Bulgarians bargain for aluminium pans. Western tourists toy with carpets, miniatures and leather goods and locals shop for their daily needs. Now more than ever, Istanbul is a triumphant market place.

Look at a map and you can immediately understand why. Istanbul sits on the straits of the Bosphorus (Boğaziçi), a fast-flowing, 19-mile-long (30km) channel that connects the Black Sea (Kara Deniz) to the Mediterranean. Two bridges now span its turbulent currents, the only crossing points between Europe and Asia. It is not surprising there has been a continuous trading settlement here since the 8th century BC, when the natural inlet of the

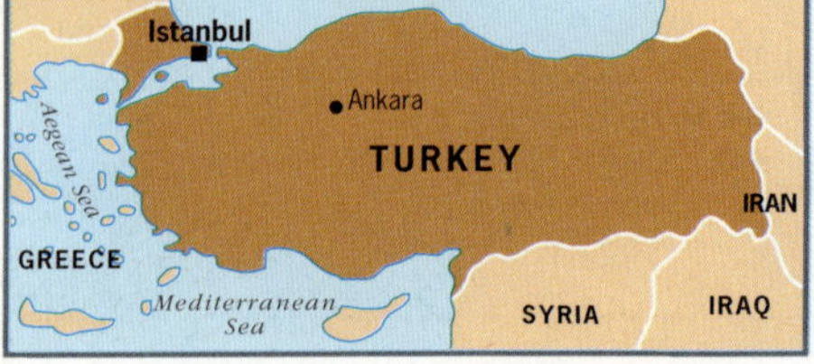

Golden Horn (Haliç) could be used as a harbour and dockyard.

Such were the advantages of the site that the city served as capital of the Byzantine Empire for a millenium and then capital of the Ottoman Empire for 500 years. It is a unique record, for no other city has been capital of a Christian and a Muslim empire consecutively. There is much that divides these periods but perhaps even more that unites them. The phenomenal buildings of Byzantine Constantinople were adapted to Ottoman use, their mysterious structure analysed and assimilated into the construction of Istanbul's magnificent domed mosques. The Byzantine architects of Ayasofya, Anthemius and Isidorus, and the great Ottoman architect Sinan seem to be joined in dialogue, not separated by a thousand years. The influence of the buildings of Istanbul can hardly be overestimated; it is one of the architectural epicentres of the world.

The city skyline is a fairytale of domes, minarets and towers, a forest of carved stone. To those arriving by sea the city announces itself proudly with the six minarets of the Blue Mosque (Sultanahmet Camii), the four of Ayasofya and the alternating domes and chimney stacks of the Topkapı Palace kitchens. Old Istanbul, like the Rome it was modelled on, was built on seven hills. These hidden contours

At peace in the mosque at Eyüp – a popular place of pilgrimage since Ottoman times

Turkish slippers

cause startling illusions: the domes and pinnacles of vast mosques suddenly disappear to be replaced by the silhouette of some previously unknown chapel. The city seems to move, to proffer yet another face to its visitors. There is one drawback to the city and that is the grey pall of diesel fumes and smog. Istanbul is no longer the capital of Turkey (which was moved to Ankara some 70 years ago) but it is still the great metropolis of the nation. The population is estimated to be around 10 million and it is growing by 350,000 a year. Pollution from cars, industry and drains continues to escalate though industries have been relocated and waterfront parks created in the city centre. However Istanbul does provide one immediate escape from noxious fumes. Get on one of the city's numerous ferries and let the sea air run fresh across your face. Riding the waterways is also such a good way to admire the city that at least one boat trip a day should be obligatory.

The most exhilarating of the trips takes all day to propel you up the Bosphorus towards the Black Sea and back. The route winds between dramatic wooded hills, elegant wooden summer houses and strategic, medieval castles, and the boat stops at a number of charming villages on the way. The fishing vessels with which the ferries share the water supply the restaurants which line the shore. There are few more fascinating places in the world to eat. The sun dances on the water as cargo ships from Bulgaria, cruise ships from Ex-Soviet republics, ferries and pleasure boats race past. Near by are glittering, white 19th-century palaces and stimulating museums.

If you have only a weekend in Istanbul, try not to miss the soaring miracle of Ayasofya, the sumptuous Iznik tiles in the Topkapı Palace, the glittering moșaics and awesome fresco in the Kariye Camii Museum, the serene classicism of the Süleymaniye Mosque and the echoing charm of the 1,500-year-old Yerebatan Sarayı cistern. Each alone is worth the trip. There is a month's worth of lesser sites in Istanbul, truly something for everyone. Go forth with energy and enjoy it.

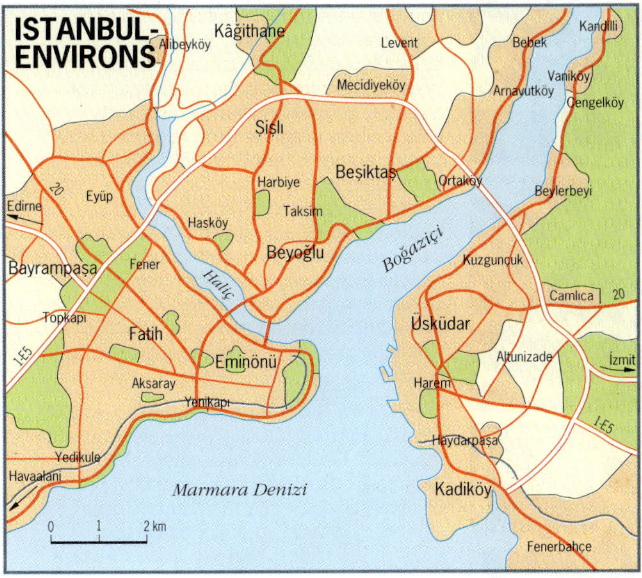

BACKGROUND

Destiny and Myth: Jason and Byzas

Istanbul was fated to be a great trading centre from the end of the Ice Age, around 40,000BC. This was when the confined waters of the Black Sea first scored out the Bosphorus (Boğaziçi) strait and flowed south into the Mediterranean. The narrow stretch of water became the vital link connecting two worlds and dividing two continents. The largest and safest harbour on the Bosphorus is the Golden Horn (Haliç), a flooded valley overlooked to the south by a peninsula that projects into the Sea of Marmara (Marmara Denizi). It is on the easternmost hill of this peninsula, known as the Acropolis but now covered by the Topkapı Palace, that Istanbul's history focuses.

Greek mythology tells of the sack of nearby Troy in the *Iliad* and the exploration of the Bosphorus and Black Sea by Jason and the Argonauts. The first brief settlement to crown the Acropolis was a 13th-century BC Mycenean colony.

This first settlement perished and was replaced centuries later by a new wave of traders. In 667BC Byzas organised an expedition recruited from two crowded and turbulent cities of Greece: Megara, his home town, and neighbouring Athens. He was guided by the cryptic advice of the Delphic Oracle to settle 'opposite the Land of the Blind'. While passing Chalcedon, modern Kadiköy, which had just been settled by a rival band of Megarans, Byzas realised that only the blind could have missed the superior opportunities offered by the Golden Horn harbour on the other shore. He promptly landed and settled the Acropolis, which became known as Byzantium in his honour.

A Pawn on the Bosphorus (667BC–AD330)

Byzantium grew into the largest and richest of the dozen Greek colonies established on the Bosphorus. However its natural benefits were continuously offset by the dangers of its strategic position, surrounded by great powers. The rulers had to pursue a flexible diplomacy of allegiance between Persia, Sparta, Athens, Boetia and Macedonia before the city passed quietly into Roman dominion. At the end of the 2nd century AD however, it supported the losing Imperial candidate, Pescennius Niger, and Emperor Septimius Severus ordered that the Acropolis be levelled and the population massacred. Within five years he thought better of his destruction and started work on a gleaming new city that was to be twice the size of the old.

Constantinople, the New Rome

In 324 Constantine destroyed Licinius, his last rival, at a battle fought within view of Byzantium in the hills above Üsküdar. Two years later he chose Byzantium as his new capital and public works soon quadrupled its size. It was officially dedicated 'New Rome' on 11 May 330 but was soon unofficially christened Constantinople.
It assumed a Christian character in opposition to pagan Rome, confirmed in 391 when Theodosius I made Christianity the state religion.
The threat of barbarian invasion coupled with the continued growth of the city led to the

construction of a new line of land walls in 447. Allied with a strong navy, this rendered the city invincible for the next thousand years, and while German tribes despoiled Rome Constantinople became the undisputed centre of the civilised Mediterranean world and Greek the language of government.
Justinian the Great dominated the 6th century from his Imperial palace here. He was determined to establish a rigid Christian Orthodoxy over his domains whilst also reconquering the lost provinces of the Roman Empire. He was assisted by a great general, Belisaurius, and by his wife Theodora, a reformed courtesan of formidable energy and ruthlessness. His efficient and highly centralised government drained the Empire of resources but the great churches he built in Constantinople, Ayasofya, St Sergius and St Bacchus (Küçük Ayasofya Camii) and Aya Irene (Aya Irini Kilise), are an exemplary testament to his visionary taste.

An Embattled Citadel (610–843)
By 610 the Empire was lost and Constantinople was under the misrule of Phocas, a violent and insane emperor. The armies of Persia and hordes of Avars, Slavs and Bulgars threatened the city. Then from Carthage came a young saviour, Heraclius, whose reign has an almost mythical quality. At first he planned to abandon the city but, bolstered by the appeals of the desperate populace, he stayed and by 641 had entirely restored the Empire's fortunes.
This was only a brief respite however, before a new and even more formidable adversary emerged out of the Arabian Desert. The Byzantine provinces of Egypt, Syria and North Africa fell to the Muslim caliphate whose Arab armies besieged Constantinople itself in 673 and 717. Bulgar armies and Slav fleets threatened from the north and the city itself was divided by the Iconoclastic Crisis. This began in 726 with an Imperial edict warning against idolatry but quickly led to the wholesale destruction of all religious imagery – icons, mosaics, paintings and frescos. The incalculable aesthetic loss to the city was mirrored by violence between the pro- and

anti-imagery parties. The dispute was finally settled by the Synod of 843 which met in Ayasofya and ruled in favour of icons.

The Heroic Age (843–1204)

The next four centuries are known as the Heroic Age, for the city was revived by a renewed interest in church building and thriving schools of monastic art. The borders of Byzantium held firm, creating a unitary state composed of modern Turkey and the Balkans south of the Danube. The apogee came during the long reign of Basil II, 976–1025, who finally destroyed the Bulgar threat. However in 1071 the entire Byzantine army was destroyed in a defile called Manzikert. At a stroke the Seljuk Turks seized Anatolia. At the same time Constantinople was losing its old commercial and naval supremacy to the Italian city states, particularly Genoa and Venice.

For a century these weaknesses were hidden by the political skills of three generations of the Comneni dynasty. Alexius I, John II and Manuel I patched together the fabric of Empire by dividing and playing off their enemies, by judicious councils, well-placed bribes and by the rapid deployment of the minimal forces at their disposal.

Decline and Two Falls (1204–1453)

However the power of the Italian merchants and mercenaries was in the ascendant. The Fourth Crusade was dominated by Dandolo, the Doge of Venice who had been blinded as a youth in Constantinople. He directed the Crusade away from its original objective and laid siege to the city. On 13 April 1204 the Crusaders breached a section of the Golden Horn seawall and sacked the city. They burnt

Medieval impressions of Istanbul, from a 14th century psalter

Fatih Mosque

what treasures they could not melt down for bullion and parcelled out the land amongst themselves. By 1261 the ruler of Byzantine Nicaea, Michael Palaeologus, was able to recapture the shattered remnants of Constantinople with the aid of the Genoese. His descendants ruled the city for the next two hundred years, presiding over a brilliant period of intellectual and artistic activity which fuelled the Italian Renaissance. However the Empire remained chronically weak, for the Genoese controlled its commerce from their self-governing colony at Galata and the provinces were governed by their own turbulent feudal dynasties.

In 1326 the Ottoman Turks established an efficiently organised state based at Bursa, only 62 miles (100km) south of Constantinople. Their capture of the European city of Adrianople (Edirne) in 1361 entirely isolated Constantinople within Ottoman territory. The final assault on the city was delayed by the Mongol invasion, but by March 1453 Sultan Mehmet II controlled the Bosphorus and had amassed a large enough army, navy and artillery force to besiege the city. After seven weeks, on 29 May, the city walls were breached and the last emperor of Byzantium, Constantine XI, perished defending them. Its citizens were slaughtered or enslaved and its treasures carried away.

The Golden Centuries of Ottoman Istanbul (1454–1683)

Mehmet II returned a year later to turn the devastated city into the capital of the Ottoman Empire. He built a residential palace at Beyazit, an administrative palace at Topkapı, rebuilt the markets and warehouses and encouraged Turks, Greeks, Armenians and Jews into the city. The great Fatih Mosque was raised over the ruins of the Church of the Holy Apostles and he encouraged his ministers to build. During the reign of Beyazit II the Ottoman navy began to wrest control of the seas from the Italians. His son Selim the Grim claimed the Muslim caliphate (leadership of the faith) after he had conquered Egypt, Syria and eastern Anatolia. The fourth Ottoman sultan to reign in Istanbul was Süleyman the Magnificent. From 1520 to

1566 he presided over the most powerful state in the world, extending it over the Aegean islands, North Africa and the whole of the Balkans. Istanbul was ornamented with a profusion of elegant mosques, baths, schools, fountains, gardens and tombs. Many were decorated with exquisite tiles produced at Iznik and were designed by Mimar Sinan, the great exponent of Ottoman classical architecture whose most celebrated work is the Süleymaniye Mosque. The seeds of decay were planted by Süleyman's wife Roxelana, who first united the residential and administrative palaces, allowing the pernicious rivalries of the harem to dominate Imperial politics. Roxelana revealed the full extent of her power by destroying Ibrahim Paşa, the hitherto omnipotent Grand Vizier and Prince Mustafa, the popular eldest son of Süleyman.

Baroque to Rococo, 1683–1909

The decline of the Ottoman Empire only became fully apparent in the failure of the 1683 siege of Vienna. Nineteen years later at the Treaty of Carlowitz, the sultan was forced to cede great swathes of territory to Russia and Austria. Shortly afterwards the court at Istanbul reached a swan-song of elegance and expenditure under the Tulip Sultan, Ahmet III. He presided over an almost continuous succession of fêtes from 1703 until his deposition in 1730. Later in the century Mustafa III commissioned his talented baroque architect, Mehmet Tahir Ağa, to create the Laleli and Ayazma mosques and to rebuild the Fatih Mosque.

It was not until the elite traditionalist standing army, the Janissaries, was massacred in the Hippodrome in 1826 that the necessary reforms to the creaking state structure could be made. The modernisation was symbolised by the adoption of Prussian military blue uniforms and a morning coat and fez, known as the 'Stambouline', at court instead of Ottoman kaftans. Sultan Abdül Mecit (1839–61) moved from the Topkapı to the newly-built rococo palace of Dolmabahçe. But the Crimean War graphically proved that the stability of the Ottoman Empire was dependent on the

Sultan Abdül Hamit II came to power in 1876 and ruled Turkey with a repressive hand for 30 years

support of France and Britain. The Tanzimat movement attempted to halt the further loss of Ottoman territory (Egypt, Tunisia, Algeria, Serbia, Greece, Romania, Montenegro and Bulgaria had by now all become independent states) by a gradual transition from the Ottoman autocracy to a liberal commonwealth of nations. However in 1878 this promising development was halted by Abdül Hamit II who went on to run a reactionary police state from his walled palace at Yıldız.

Atatürk and the Turkish Republic

In 1909 the 'Young Turk' coup deposed Abdül Hamit II and replaced him with a military dictatorship ruling through a puppet sultan. By 1919 the Allied powers had stripped the Empire of its remaining provinces and French and British cruisers and cavalry patrolled the Bosphorus strait and the streets of Istanbul. When Sultan Mehmet VI agreed to the partitioning of western Anatolia amongst the Greeks and Italians, Mustafa Kemal Atatürk, the heroic commander of Gallipoli, left Istanbul to raise the standard of revolt.

Within three years Atatürk had defeated and expelled the foreign armies beyond the present frontiers of the Turkish Republic. He then began the task of transforming Turkey into a westernised secular state. The office of sultan was abolished, Atatürk moved the capital inland to Ankara and took the dramatic step of abolishing the Muslim caliphate in 1924. Next the influential Dervish brotherhoods were outlawed and the Kurds and doctors of

Dome of Sokullu Mehmet Paşa

religious law humbled. Urban women were given a measure of emancipation and the Roman alphabet was adopted. Istanbul, deprived of the status and revenues of a capital, sank into a depression that only lifted in the 1960s. The city has now revived, thanks partly to new motorways and two magnificent bridges over the Bosphorus. Its unique collection of monuments is being restored, coastal parks are being created and commercial confidence has returned. A third of the population of Turkey now lives in Greater Istanbul.

Top Turks

Many of the great officials of the Ottoman Empire retired to Istanbul. They erected sumptuous town houses and elegant wooden palaces (*yalis*) overlooking the Bosphorus. Only a few of these have survived, and the officials' most lasting memorials are mostly their mausolea (*türbe*), and mosques, public fountains and charitable institutions which they endowed.

At the summit of the hierarchy was the *Sultan*, a specifically Turkish word which meant the sovereign ruler. His other title, *Caliph*, presented his claim to be the single ruler of the entire Muslim world and successor to the authority of the prophet Mohammed. His four wives were referred to as *Sultana*, though it was his mother, the *Valide Sultan*, who was the most powerful woman in the Empire. The *divan*, the ruling council of the Empire, was composed of the various ministers, or *viziers*, and chief judges, *cadis*, and was presided over by the *Grand Vizier*. Also influential were the *agas*, the commanders of the palace eunuchs and Jannisary guards. The Imperial provinces and lesser military campaigns were directed by *paşas*, who were ranked one, two or three horse tails, and carried the appropriate number of horse-tail banners. A *bey* was the governor of a district and a *dey*, literally a maternal uncle, was an officer in command of a hundred men. Outside this strict hierarchy were the honorary titles of *gazi*, a warrior of the Muslim faith and *haçi*, a pilgrim returned from Mecca.

What to See

The Essential rating system:

✓ 'top ten'

◆◆◆ do not miss
◆◆ see if you can
◆ worth seeing if you have time

AREAS OF THE CITY

Once you master the ferry boats and realise how cheap and fast the city's yellow taxis are you can dart all over Istanbul in a day. We have followed the current boundaries that divide central Istanbul into three areas: Eminönü, Fatih and Beyoğlu. The second suspension bridge, Fatih Sultan Mehmet, on the Bosphorus (Boğaziçi) is an obvious division between the upper and lower reaches of the waterway.

Eminönü
On a brief visit it will be difficult to tear yourself away from Eminönü which covers the eastern half of Old Istanbul. Practically all the great attractions are here: Ayasofya, the Topkapı Palace, the Blue Mosque (Sultanahmet Camii), Beyazit Mosque, Archaeological Museum, Yerebatan Sarayı, the Süleymaniye Mosque and the Covered Bazaar. It also contains most of the interesting hotels, Turkish baths (*hamam*), carpet shops, many cheap restaurants and dozens of lesser sites.

Fatih
The western half of Old Istanbul is named after Fatih Camii, the Mosque of Victory which lies at its heart, and was built by Mehmet II, the conqueror of Constantinople.
Fatih is comparatively empty of tourists though the castle of Yediküle, Kariye Camii Museum in Chora, Eyüp Mosque and the Theodosian walls should be on your itinerary. For those with time, there are a dozen intriguing minor sites.

Beyoğlu
Opposite Old Istanbul, on the far shore of the Golden Horn (Haliç), rises the cubist skyline of Beyoğlu, a jumble of offices and apartments pierced by the silhouette of the Galata Tower. The tower with its fabulous view is easily the most popular monument, while other lesser sites include the Military Museum, the Municipal Art Gallery, the Mevlevi Tekke (Monastery of the Whirling Dervishes) and half a dozen elusive mosques along the shore. Beyoğlu is visited not so much for these as for the

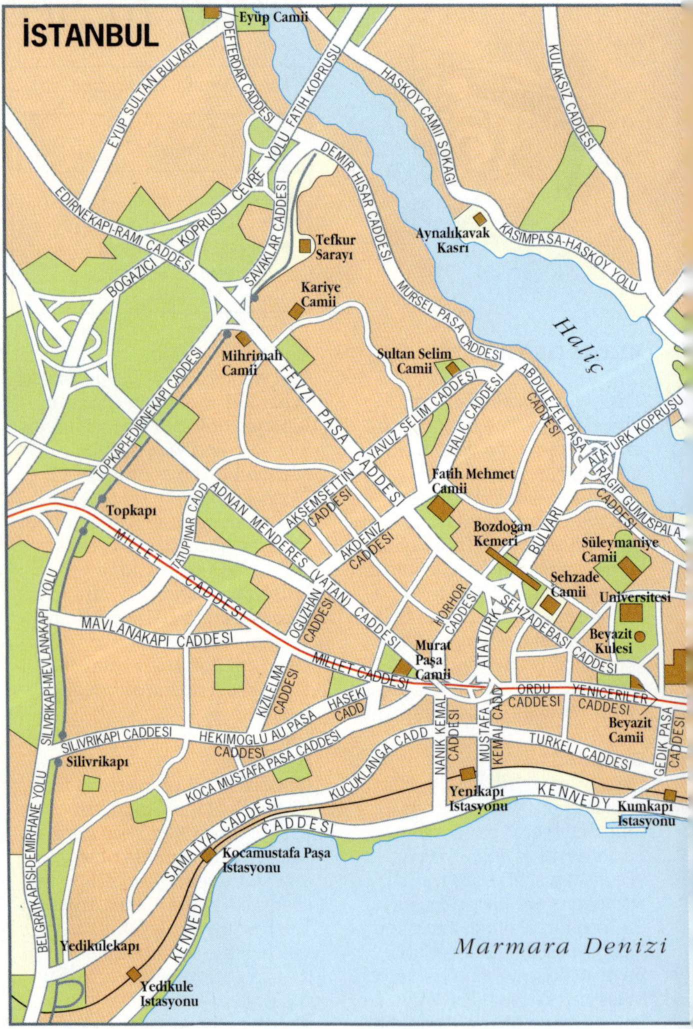
İSTANBUL
Eyüp Camii
EYÜP SULTAN BULVARI
DEFTERDAR CADDESI
FATIH KOPRUSU
HASKOY CAMII SOKAGI
KULAKSIZ CADDESI
DEMIR HISAR CADDESI
CEVRE YOLU
EDIRNEKAPI-RAMI CADDESI
BOGAZICI KOPRUSU
SAVAKLAR CADDESI
Tefkur Sarayı
Aynalıkavak Kasrı
KASIMPASA-HASKOY YOLU
Kariye Camii
MURSEL PASA CADDESI
Haliç
Mihrimah Camii
Sultan Selim Camii
FEVZI PASA CADDESI
TOPKAPI-EDIRNEKAPI CADDESI
YAVUZ SELIM CADDESI
HALIC CADDESI
ABDULEZEL PASA CADDESI
ATATURK KOPRUSU
Fatih Mehmet Camii
RAGIP GUMUSPALA CADDESI
Topkapı
ADNAN MENDERES (VATAN) CADDESI
AKSEMSETTIN CADDESI
AKDENIZ CADDESI
Bozdoğan Kemeri
BULVARI
Süleymaniye Camii
TATUPINAR CADD
MILLET CADDESI
Şehzade Camii
Universitesi
HORHOR CADDESI
SEHZADEBASI CADDESI
Beyazit Kulesi
ATATURK
MEVLANAKAPI CADDESI
OGUZHAN CADDESI
Murat Paşa Camii
MILLET CADDESI
ORDU CADDESI
YENICERILER CADDESI
KIZILELMA CADDESI
HASEKI CADD
NANIK KEMAL CADDESI
MUSTAFA KEMAL CADD
Beyazit Camii
SILIVRIKAPI-MEVLANAKAPI YOLU
SILIVRIKAPI CADDESI
HEKIMOGLU ALI PASA CADDESI
TURKELI CADDESI
GEDIK PASA CADDESI
Silivrikapı
KOCA MUSTAFA PASA CADDESI
KUCUKLANGA CADD
Yenikapı Istasyonu
KENNEDY
Kumkapı Istasyonu
BELGRATKAPISI-DEMIRHANE YOLU
SAMATYA CADDESI
CADDESI
Kocamustafa Paşa Istasyonu
KENNEDY
Marmara Denizi
Yedikulekapı
Yedikule Istasyonu

Atatürk Müzesi
Askeri Müzesi
Yıldız Parkı
PIYALE PAŞA BULVARI
DOLAPDERE CADDESI
CUMHURIYET CADDESI
KADIRGALAR CADDESI
BARBAROS BULVARI
ÇIRAĞAN CADDESI
DOLMABAHÇE CADDESI
Deniz Müzesi
Beşiktaş Vapur Iskelesi
Resim ve Heykel Müzesi
Dolmabahçe Sarayı
İnönü Stadyumu
Atatürk Kültür Merkezi
Taksim Meydanı
INÖNÜ CADDESI
Dolmabahçe Saat Kulesi
Dolmabahçe Camii
Kabataş Vapur Iskelesi
BEYOĞLU
HAYAM CADDESI
OMER
SAYDAM CADDESI
REFIK
ISTIKLAL
YENICARSI CADDESI
SIRASELVILER CADDESI
MECLISIMEBUSAN CADDESI
Boğaziçi
Galata Kulesi
KEMERALTI CADDESI
NECATIBEY CADDESI
VOYVODA CADDESI
TERSANE CADDESI
GALATA KÖPRÜSÜ
Mihrimah Camii
Semsı Ahmet Paşa Camii
Rumi Mehmet Paşa Camii
Yeni Valide Camii
Kız Kulesi
Ayazma Camii
DOĞANCILAR CADDESI
HALK CADDESI
ÜSKÜDAR
Rüstem Paşa Camii
Yeni Camii
REŞADIYE CADDESI
Sirkeci Istasyon
Atatürk Heykeli
KENNEDY CADDESI
Gotlar Sütunu
Mısır Çarşısı
HAMIDIYE CADD
Arkeoloji Müzesi
Kapalıçarşı
ANKARA CADD
Vilayet Porte
Gülhane Parkı
Topkapı Sarayı
Çemberlitaş
Yerebatan Sarayı
Aya Irini Kilisesi
Ahmet III Çeşmesı
DIVAN YOLU CADDESI
Ayasofya
AT MEYDANI
Adiye Sarayı
Sultanahmet Camii
Cankurtaran Istasyonu
CADDESI
Selimiye Camii
Harem Feribot Iskelesi
ISTANBUL ANKARA DEVLET YOLU
Selimiye Kışlası
0
500
1000 m

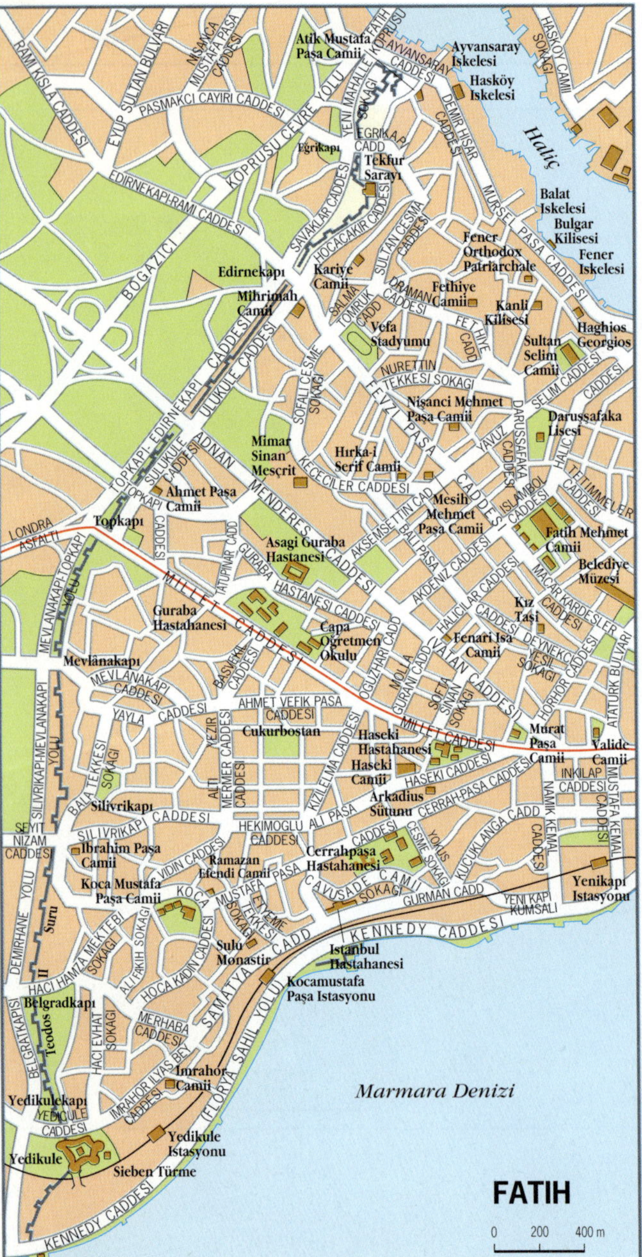

FATIH
0
200
400 m
Marmara Denizi
Haliç
Atik Mustafa Paşa Camii
Ayvansaray Iskelesi
Hasköy Iskelesi
Eğrikapı
Tekfur Sarayı
Balat Iskelesi
Bulgar Kilisesi
Fener Iskelesi
Fener Orthodox Patriarchale
Fethiye Camii
Kanli Kilisesi
Haghios Georgios
Sultan Selim Camii
Edirnekapı
Kariye Camii
Mihrimah Camii
Vefa Stadyumu
Nişanci Mehmet Paşa Camii
Darussafaka Lisesi
Mimar Sinan Mescrit
Hırka-i Serif Camii
Mesih Mehmet Paşa Camii
Ahmet Paşa Camii
Topkapı
Fatih Mehmet Camii
Belediye Müzesi
Asagi Guraba Hastanesi
Guraba Hastahanesi
Capa Ogretmen Okulu
Kız Taşi
Fenari Isa Camii
Mevlânakapı
Cukurbostan
Haseki Hastahanesi
Haseki Camii
Murat Paşa Camii
Valide Camii
Arkadius Sütunu
Silivrikapı
Ibrahim Paşa Camii
Ramazan Efendi Camii
Cerrahpaşa Hastahanesi
Koca Mustafa Paşa Camii
Yenikapi Istasyonu
Sulu Mønastir
Istanbul Hastahanesi
Kocamustafa Paşa Istasyonu
Belgradkapı
Imrahor Camii
Yedikulekapı
Yedikule Istasyonu
Yedikule
Sieben Türme
Mermer Kule
II Teodos Suru
RAMI KISLA CADDESI
EYUP SULTAN BULVARI
NISANCA MUSTAFA PASA CADDESI
PASMAKCI CAYIRI CADDESI
KOPRUSU CEVRE YOLU
FATIH KOPRUSU
AYVANSARAY CADDESI
YENI MAHALLE SOKAGI
EGRIKAPI CADD
DEMIRHISAR CADDESI
HASKOY CAMII SOKAGI
EDIRNEKAPI-RAMI CADDESI
SAVAKLAR CADDESI
HOCACAKIR CADDESI
SULTAN CESMA CADDESI
MURSEL PASA CADDESI
BOGAZICI
DRAMAN CADDESI
SALMA TOMRUK CADD
FETHIYE CADD
EDIRNEKAPI CADDESI
ULUKULE CADDESI
SOFALI CESME SOKAGI
NURETTIN TEKKESI SOKAGI
FEVZI PASA CADDESI
SELIM CADDESI
TOPKAPI-EDIRNEKAPI
SULUKULE CADDESI
ADNAN MENDERES CADDESI
KECECILER CADDESI
YAVUZ
DARUSSAFAKA CADDESI
HALICI
TETIMMELER
ISLAMBOL CADDESI
AKSEMSETTIN CAD
BALI PASA
LONDRA ASFALTI
TOPKAPI CADDESI
TATUPINAR CADD
GURABA HASTANESI CADDESI
AKDENIZ CADDESI
MACAR KARDESLER CADDESI
MEVLANAKAPI-TOPKAPI YOLU
MILLET CADDESI
HALICILAR CADDESI
DEYNEKCI
YESIL SOKAGI
HORHOR CADDESI
ATATURK BULVARI
BASVEKIL CADDESI
OGUZHAN CADD
MOLLA GURANI CADD
VATAN CADDESI
SOFTA SINAN SOKAGI
MEVLANAKAPI CADDESI
AHMET VEFIK PASA CADDESI
YAYLA CADDESI
YEZIR
SILIVRIKAPI-MEVLANAKAPI YOLU
BALA TEKKESI SOKAGI
MERMER CADDESI
ALTI MERMER CADDESI
KIZILELMA CADDESI
HASEKI CADDESI
CERRAH-PASA CADDESI
INKILAP CADDESI
NAMIK KEMAL CADDESI
MUSTAFA KEMAL CADDESI
SEYIT NIZAM CADDESI
SILIVRIKAPI CADDESI
HEKIMOGLU ALI PASA CADDESI
CESME SOKAGI
YOKUS
KUCUKLANGA CADD
VIDIN CADDESI
CAVUSADE CAMII SOKAGI
GURMAN CADD
YENI KAPI KUMSALI
DEMIRHANE YOLU
KOCA MUSTAFA PASA
ETYEME TEKKESI SOKAGI
KENNEDY CADDESI
HACI HAMZA MEKTEBI SOKAGI
ALI FAKIH SOKAGI
HOCA KADIN CADDESI
SAMATYA CADD
BELGRATKAPISI
HACI EVHAT SOKAGI
MERHABA CADDESI
IMRAHOR ILYAS BEY CADDESI
FLORYA SAHIL YOLU
YEDICULE CADDESI
KENNEDY CADDESI

glamorous hotels at Taksim and for Istiklal Caddesi, the main shopping avenue whose side streets are lined with restaurants, nightclubs, seedy bars, consulates and churches.

The Lower Bosphorus
Every day in Istanbul should include at least one ferry journey. The romantic views, fresh air and the choice of fish restaurants alone require it. In addition you can ricochet up the various ferry routes of the lower Bosphorus to visit the castle of Rumeli Hisarı, the markets and quietly elegant mosques of Üsküdar, Ortaköy and Selimiye and the four 19th-century Imperial palaces: Dolmabahçe, Beylerbey, Yıldız and Küçüksu.

The Upper Bosphorus and Excursions
Trips which take up the whole day include one to the fishing villages along the upper Bosphorus or those to the Princes' Islands (Kizil Adalar), the Belgrade Forest (Belgrad Ormani) and the sandy resorts of the Black Sea. Trips further afield, to ski at Uludağ or to the mountain haven Lake Abant, make a refreshing two-day break from what can be an exhausting city.

Turkish terms

cami(i)	mosque
çarşı	bazaar, market
hisar(ı)	Ottoman fortress
iskele	boat landing stage
kapı	gate
kilise	church
kösk(ü)	kiosk or pavilion
saray(ı)	Ottoman palace
türbe	Ottoman mausoleum

(See also **Language** page 124.)

Afloat along the Bosphorus

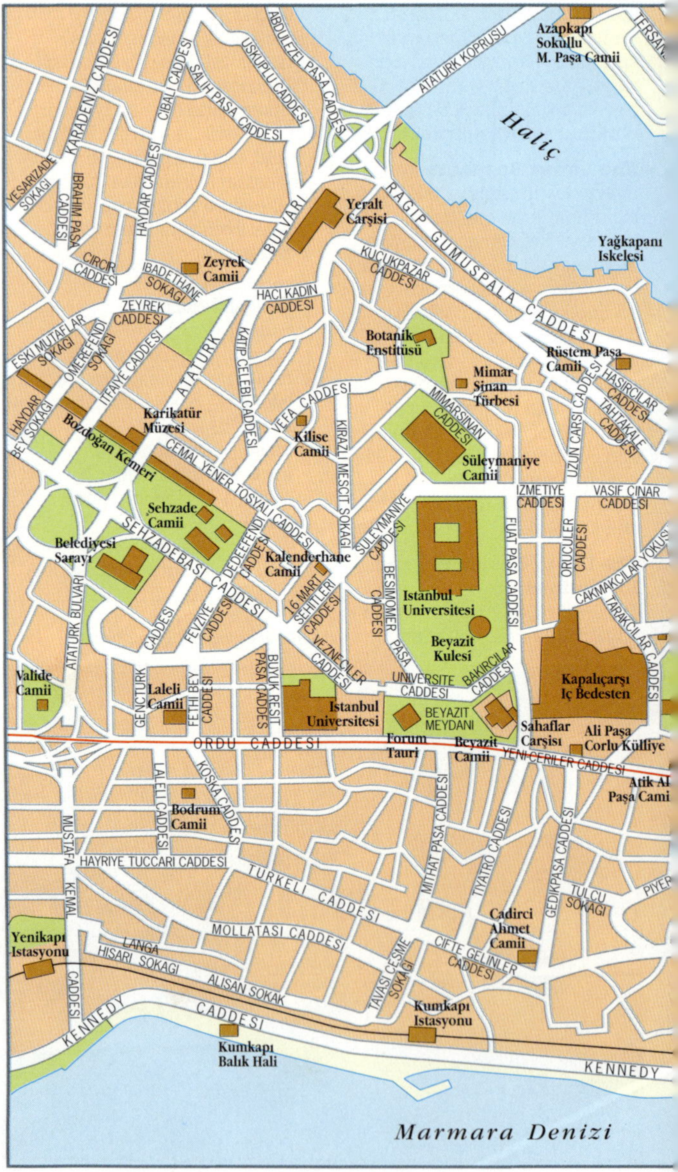
Azapkapı
Sokullu
M. Paşa Camii
Haliç
Yeralt
Çarşisi
Yağkapanı
Iskelesi
Zeyrek
Camii
Botanik
Enstitüsü
Rüstem Paşa
Camii
Mimar
Sinan
Türbesi
Karikatür
Müzesi
Bozdoğan Kemeri
Kilise
Camii
Süleymaniye
Camii
Sehzade
Camii
Belediyesi
Sarayı
Kalenderhane
Camii
Istanbul
Universitesi
Beyazit
Kulesi
Kapalıçarşı
Iç Bedesten
Valide
Camii
Laleli
Camii
Istanbul
Universitesi
BEYAZIT
MEYDANI
Sahaflar
Çarşısı
Ali Paşa
Corlu Külliye
Forum
Tauri
Beyazit
Camii
Bodrum
Camii
Cadirci
Ahmet
Camii
Yenikapı
Istasyonu
Kumkapı
Istasyonu
Kumkapı
Balık Hali
Marmara Denizi
ATATURK KOPRUSU
RAGIP GUMUSPALA CADDESI
ORDU CADDESI
YENI CERILER CADDESI
TURKELI CADDESI
MOLLATASI CADDESI
HAYRIYE TUCCARI CADDESI
KENNEDY CADDESI
CIFTE GELINLER CADDESI
ALISAN SOKAK
LANGA HISARI SOKAGI

CENTRAL İSTANBUL
EMINÖNÜ
Boğaziçi
Arap Camii
Tünel
Yeraltı Camii
Haliç Iskelesi
Karaköy Vapur Iskelesi
VOYVODA CADDESI
KEMERALTI CADDESI
NECATI BEY CADDESI
KEMANKES CADDESI
RIHTIM CADDESI
GALATA KOPRUSU
Sarayburnu
Yeni Camii
Eminönü Iskelesi
Sirkeci Iskelesi
Atatürk Heykeli
RESADIYE CADDESI
KENNEDY CADDESI
Sirkeci Istasyonu
Mısır Çarşısı
HAMIDIYE CADDESI
SEHINSAH PEHLEVI CADDESI
ASIR EFENDI CADDESI
MURADIYE CADDESI
Gotlar Sütunu
Gülhane Parkı
Tanzimat Müzesi
HUDAVENIGAR CADDESI
EBUSSUUT CADDESI
CEMAL NADIR SOKAGI
SULTAN MEKTEBI SOKAGI
ANKARA
Harem
Topkapı Sarayı
Cinili Köşkü
Vilayet
TURKOCAGI CADDESI
Eski Sark Eserleri Müzesi
Arkeoloji Müzesi
Mahmut Paşa Camii
ALEMDAR CADDESI
Aya Irini Kilisesi
Caferağa Medrese
CATAL CESME SOKAGI
YEREBATAN CADDESI
BABIALI CADDESI
Çemberlitaş
Sağlık Müzesi
Ahmet III Çeşmesi
DIVAN YOLU CADDESI
Yerebatan Sarayı
Sultan Mahmut II Türbesi
AYASOFYA MEYDANI
Ayasofya
Firuz Ağa Camii
Adiye Sarayı
Fener
Gülhane Hastahanesi
PEYK HANE SOKAGI
Hippodrome
AT MEYDANI
Roxelana Hamamı
ISHAKPASA CADDESI
Sultanahmet Camii ve Türbesi
Halı Müzesi
AKBIYIK CADDESI
Ibraham Paşa Sarayı
Türk Islam Eserleri Müzesi
OZBEKLER SOKAGI
KABASAKAL CADDESI
Cankurtaran Istasyonu
Sokullu Mehmet Paşa Camii
Mozaik Müzesi
Küçük Ayasofya Camii
AKSAKAL SOKAGI
MUSTAFA PASA SOKAGI
CANKURTARAN
CADDESI
0
200
400 m

◆◆
AHMET III ÇEŞMESI (FOUNTAIN OF AHMET III)

Babihumayun Caddesi, entrance to Topkapı Palace, Eminönü

In 1730 the aesthetic and extravagant Ahmet III was deposed and many of his finest follies destroyed. Luckily this magnificent rococo fountain survived. Spring water once flowed into the four side basins, while from the protruding grilled *sebils* (counters) on the corners, assistants served sherbets and flavoured waters in ice-chilled silver goblets. The projecting leaded roof casts shade over the poet Seyit Vehbi Efendi's dedicatory verse which reveals the fountain's date in the sum of the numerical values of its initial letters.

◆◆
ALI PAŞA ÇORLU KÜLLIYE

36 and 36A Yeniçeriler Caddesi, Eminönü

This *külliye* or pious foundation is now occupied by two carpet shops, one of which operates opposite a picturesque tea garden complete with an array of water pipes. The latter is reached through a small walled cemetery into one half of the *medrese* courtyard – the other half and the entrance to the mosque is at 36A. The *külliye* was built in the first decade of the 18th century by Ali Paşa, a son-in-law of Mustafa II who was exiled to Lesbos by the succeeding sultan and eventually executed. His well-connected family managed to survive the disgrace and

placed the Paşa's severed head in his prepared tomb.
Open: hours of prayer; carpet shops closed Sunday.

◆
ANADOLU HISARI

Asian shore of the lower Bosphorus
Opposite the mighty towers of Rumeli Hisarı is the small fortress of Anadolu Hisarı (Anatolian castle), built by Sultan Beyazit I in 1390. Sixty-three years later the two forts cut Constantinople off from her corn supply on the Black Sea, as a precursor to the Ottoman conquest of the city. There is a stairway up to the keep, but the castle's romance is diminished by the coast road that runs through its outer bailey. The river just below the castle combined with the Küçüksu stream in cleaner centuries to form the Sweet Waters of Asia, a favourite spot for picnics and promenades.

◆
ARAP CAMII (THE ARAB MOSQUE)

Abdusselah Sokaği, Beyoğlu
Only the brick and stone exterior, the belfry and the long nave divided into three hint at this mosque's Christian origins. The interior galleries, wooden columns and ogee windows are all later Islamic additions. It started life as a 14th-century Dominican church within Genoese Galata. It was converted into a mosque in the 16th century for the use of the Andalucian refugees who settled here after the fall of Muslim Granada.
Open: hours of prayer.

◆◆◆
ARKEOLOJI MÜZESI ✓ (ARCHAEOLOGICAL MUSEUM)

Between Topkapı Palace and Gülhane Park, Eminönü
This remarkable national collection is currently in various stages of reorganisation, but the museum complex divides roughly into four. Those with little time should head for the ground floor of the main building and its stunning display of sarcophagi and classical sculptures. The nearby Museum of the Ancient Orient has a rich and diverse collection, but is badly lit and arranged. The magnificent collection of Islamic ceramics in the 15th-century Çinili Köşkü is surrounded by outdoor carvings and the tables of a café.

The Sarcophagi
A vast statue of the god Bes, from Cyprus, greets visitors at the entrance hall. To the left are the sarcophagi rooms: a quite exceptional and dramatic display which begins with a pair of 6th-century BC Egyptian and a pair of 5th-century BC Phoenician sarcophagi. The arched corpse of the Phoenician King Tabnit of Sidon occupied the sarcophagus that had been carved a century earlier for an Egyptian general. Hieroglyphics cover its surface except at the feet where it is replaced by the Phoenician script. Beyond the stairs, where an exhibition commemorates the life of Osman Hamdi Bey,

discoverer of these tombs and creator of the museum, lies the culmination of the display: the Alexander Sarcophagus and the tomb of the mourning women, carved between 350 and 300BC. These superb tombs, modelled on contemporary temples, have preserved architectural details in their meticulously carved cornices, friezes and gargoyles. The Alexander Sarcophagus was made for a prince of the Macedonian Seleucid dynasty not for the great man himself, though Alexander appears twice in the carvings. In the furious battle scene between Greeks and Persians he is the mounted figure on the extreme left wearing a lion-skin headdress. Now spot the king in the hunting scene!

Archaeological Museum

Classical Sculpture

The classical sculpture galleries fill eight ground-floor rooms to the right of the entrance hall. They exhibit over 1,000 years of sculpture (800BC–AD400) discovered all over the Ottoman Empire, with good explanatory texts in Turkish and English and excellent dramatic lighting. Walking through the centuries, the faces become increasingly realistic and culminate in the portrait busts of historical figures from ancient Rome in the sixth room. Three heads of Augustus begin the gallery of emperors. The cold beauty of Agrippina the elder has been placed between Tiberius and Claudius, her brother-in-law and nephew. From Crete comes the propaganda image of Hadrian treading a barbarian underfoot. From one corner comes the disdainful gaze of Marcus Aurelius, the philosopher emperor and his reprobate colleague, Lucius Verus. The heavy, bearded head of the crowned Diocletian perfectly fits his image as a tough and conscientious soldier.

The Upper Floor Galleries
The long gallery on the first floor takes on two vast themes: on the right, the story of Troy from 3000BC to the Roman Empire; on the left, the story of Anatolia from 10,000 to 546BC. This takes you through the beginnings of agriculture and bronze working, to the time when Indo-European migration and Assyrian influences produced the Hittite Empire of eastern Anatolia. It culminates in the Lydian and Phrygian kingdoms before their conquest by Persia in the 6th century BC.
The second-floor gallery continues to focus on prehistory with parallel exhibitions tracking the cultures of Cyprus and Syria-Palestine to the Roman period. One room is devoted to Parthian carving and the distinctive, green-glazed, slipper-shaped sarcophagi of this nomadic dynasty that ruled Persia from 200BC to AD220. The gallery culminates in a mausoleum created to display the museum's extensive collection of portrait busts from Palmyra.

The Museum of the Ancient Orient
This museum contains antiquities from early civilisations – Sumer, Babylon, Assyria, Egypt and Hittite Anatolia. A pair of Hittite lions flanks the entrance. Upstairs to the left lie the four wooden and plastered mummies (1200–935BC) at the heart of the museum's Egyptian collection. The Mesopotamian hall is dominated by the magnificent glazed brick friezes on the walls produced in the New Babylonian Empire of 625–539BC. The bull of Adad, the dragon of Marduk and the lion of Ishtar once decorated the walls of a sacred road leading from Babylon's Ishtar gate to the temple of the New Year. The striking glazed colours – blue, turquoise, white and yellow – are still favourite colours for the religious buildings of the Middle East.
The rest of the collection includes the other great early Mesopotamian civilisations: Sumer and Assyria. From Sumer (3200–2800BC) come the reed-skirted figures, clay tiles stamped with man's earliest writing and the Buddha-like calm of Gudea, a priest-king. Assyrian relief-carved tablets, mostly from the aggressive, 9th-century period, lead towards the rougher basalt carving of the Hittites. Look out for the earliest treaty of mankind, the Peace of Kadesh between the Egyptian and Hittite Empires in 1269BC, a copy of which stands as a memorial in the foyer of the UN building. Also from Babylonian temples come a standard measuring stick and the bewitchingly elegant, duck-shaped, 66-pound (30kg) weight.

The Çinili Köşkü (housing the Museum of Turkish Ceramics)
The köşk itself is the oldest secular Islamic building in Istanbul. It was built in 1472 for Mehmet II as a pavilion from which to watch his young squires play polo. The columns and balustrade of the front

Iznik Tiles
The ceramics of Iznik are one of the great artistic glories of the Muslim world. They can be appreciated in many of the Ottoman monuments of Istanbul.
Iznik, a small walled town 115 miles (185km) south of Istanbul, first emerged as a centre of excellence in about AD1500, producing copies of Chinese and Persian blue and white porcelain. As the century progressed an increasingly confident and innovative style emerged and new colours enhanced the repertoire: turquoise, green and a misty purple picked out by delicate black outlines. In about 1550, during the reign of Süleyman the Magnificent, a new pigment, the famous Armenian bole, added a bold splash of tomato red to the designs. The next 50 years witnessed the golden period of Iznik ware, when the products were traded throughout the Empire and in Europe.
The influence of Istanbul's palace architects and painting workshop encouraged a late 16th-century flowering of naturalistic motifs: carnations, tulips, roses and hyacinths.
At first, these tiles were produced just for specific Imperial commissions, but as demand grew so too did production. Perhaps because of this dilution of effort, after 1600 Iznik ware went into a rapid and mysterious decline, becoming increasingly weak and derivative.

gallery are 19th-century restorations but the rest of the building, decorated with ceramic inlays, is original. It houses a small but fine collection of Iznik tiles, lamps and Seljuk pottery.

The Outdoor Carvings
Pride of place belongs to the four Byzantine Imperial sarcophagi that were carved from solid blocks of Egyptian porphyry – the purple Stone of Kings. They are modestly uninscribed, except for the Christian monograms in Greek of PX and Alpha-Omega.
Open: 09.30–17.00hrs. *Closed:* Monday. Admission charge. Photography charge.

◆

ASKERI MÜZESI (MILITARY MUSEUM)

Spor ve Sergi Sarayı Çarşısı, Harbiye, Beyoğlu
The best aspect of this well-signposted museum is the band dressed in the uniform of the Janissaries, which plays stirring military music and sings rousing marching songs from 15.00 to 16.00hrs every afternoon the museum is open. Otherwise the museum divides between an opulent nationalistic shrine to the heroes of the Turkish nation, and an older, dustier display of military uniforms and portraits. In the former there are some magnificent Imperial campaign tents and Ottoman horse-hair standards to be seen. In the latter, do not miss the preserved length of the Byzantine chain that sealed the Golden Horn.
Open: 09.00–17.00hrs. *Closed:* Monday and Tuesday.

◆◆◆

AT MEYDANI (HIPPODROME)

Beside Sultanahmet, Eminönü

This long garden square studded by monuments and overlooked by the Blue Mosque is an extraordinary historical survival. The surrounding tarmac road closely follows the chariot racetrack built by the Emperor Septimius Severus in the 2nd century AD. To the east stood the royal box which communicated directly with the palace of the Byzantine emperors. This meeting of monarch and masses made the Hippodrome the political nerve centre through the long centuries of Byzantium. The ruins continued to serve as a parade and execution ground during the Ottoman Empire. One can but hope that the sum total of revolutions, *coups*, public executions and massacres of 2000 years might yet be equalled by parades, celebrations, rallies and races. On the site of the present tourist information office there once stood an ornamental tower, crowned by the celebrated bronze horses of San Marco which were looted from here by the Venetians in the Fourth Crusade. The next monument on what would have been a raised central terrace is the German fountain, the only ugly fountain in Istanbul but one of the few in working order. It is a lumpen copy of the fountain in the Blue Mosque and was built to mark the visit of Kaiser Wilhelm II in 1898. In the domed ceiling the Kaiser's monogram alternates with the *tuğra* (calligraphic monogram) of Abdül Hamid II.

Continuing southwest, the hieroglyphics on the Egyptian granite obelisk could have been carved yesterday. In fact the obelisk is 16th century BC, made to commemorate a successful campaign in

Egyptian obelisk at the Hippodrome

northern Syria. Two thousand years later it was shipped to Istanbul but broke into pieces at the docks. This is merely the top third; it was placed here by the Emperor Theodosius I in AD390 on the four brazen blocks and carved marble base you see today. On its south face, the Imperial family watch a chariot race, on the west they receive the submission of barbarians, on the north Theodosius directs the raising of the obelisk and on the east he crowns the winner of a race.

More venerable still is the bronze column of three entwined snakes next door. Made from Persian armour captured by the victorious Greeks at the battle of Plataea in 479BC, it stood as a thanksgiving to Apollo at Delphi for the resulting Greek independence, until Constantine the Great took it east to grace his new city. Turkish miniatures show that it was only decapitated in the 18th century, by drunken European souvenir hunters.

The last monument, known as the brazen obelisk, was also erected by Theodosius I in 390. It was sheathed in bronze plates embossed with rural and picturesque scenes. On the summit was the winds' attendant, a gilt female figure so delicately poised that she turned with the slightest breath of wind. The bronze reliefs were ripped off and melted down for bullion during the sack of the city by the Fourth Crusade and the stone structure was later used as a perilous climbing frame by young Janissaries testing each others' bravura.

The public park to the north, above the Sultan Sofra café, is adorned with a few ruins, traces of two adjoining 5th-century palaces that belonged to the courtiers Antiochus and Lausus. They were burnt down a century later during the Nike riot and were replaced by a shrine to St Euphemia, who was martyred during Diocletian's persecution of Christians in 303.

◆

ATATÜRK MÜZESI (ATATÜRK MUSEUM)

Halaskargazi Caddesi, Şişli

Atatürk, the creator of modern Turkey, acquired this three-storey house in 1918 and lived here with his mother, sister and step-sister whilst conducting the covert negotiations with other nationalists that brought about the 1919 revolution. The display of original documents, photographs and personal belongings is only really of interest to specialist historians.

Open: Monday to Friday 09.00–12.00hrs, 13.00–15.00hrs. *Closed:* 15th of every month.

◆

ATIK ALI PAŞA CAMII

Yeniçeriler Caddesi, Eminönü

This, one of the city's oldest mosques, stands on a quiet garden terrace above the car-park below Constantine's Column. It was built in 1496 by the eunuch Grand Vizier of Beyazit II, at the centre of a complex that included a charity kitchen, a Sufi monastery and a religious college. The outer

porch leads directly into a T-shaped prayer hall. The mosque's most striking feature is the powerfully sculpted stone squinches that flank, and almost overwhelm, the mihrab.
Open: hours of prayer.

◆◆
AYA IRINI KILISE/HAGHIA EIRENE (THE CHURCH OF DIVINE PEACE)

In the first courtyard of Topkapı Palace, Eminönü

The Church of Divine Peace we see today is at least the third church on this, the oldest site of Christian worship in Istanbul. It was built in AD537 by the Emperor Justinian, at the same time as Ayasofya, but was never converted into a mosque as it was included within the walls of the Topkapı Palace and used as a military arsenal until the 19th century.

In no way does the brick and stone exterior prepare you for the magnificence of the church's interior, viewed in diffused half-light. Most of the mosaic decoration has fallen, revealing the vast, brick vaults of the central nave, supporting a window-pierced dome. The first floor gallery was integral to the original design though its assorted columns belong to an 8th-century restoration.

Most magnificent of all in this vast spiritual space is the remaining apse mosaic, a great iconoclastic cross set against a golden background which projects its serene assurance down the nave. The apse is framed by two biblical inscriptions in Greek bordered by a decorative frieze of gold crosses set in blue lozenges. The officiating clergy sat on the five banks of seats in the apse. The tunnel beneath the seats connects the aisles and dampens the echo. At the west end of the church five doors lead out into a courtyard, much altered over the centuries, but the only Byzantine courtyard to have survived in the city. The porphyry tombs of Imperial Byzantine were brought here in the mid-19th century when Aya Irini served as a museum of antiquities.
Open: periodically, when in use for exhibitions or concerts.

Traditional Turkish strategy: backgammon

♦♦♦ AYASOFYA/ HAGHI SOPHIA ✓ (THE CHURCH OF DIVINE WISDOM)

Ayasofya Meydani, Sultanahmet, Eminönü

In the last months of his 36-year reign, the aged Emperor Justinian led a procession of citizens, at dawn on Christmas Eve in 563, to inaugurate the Church of Divine Wisdom. He paused to exclaim: 'Glory be to God, who has thought me worthy of accomplishing such a work. Oh Solomon, I have surpassed you.'

Ayasofya is one of the great buildings of the world. Its age, historical importance and enormous architectural influence assure it of that. Built as a church in the 6th century, converted to a mosque in the 15th, Ayasofya in the 20th century has become a museum. The last thing you expect is that it will still surprise, and yet no photograph or description can prepare you for the first impact of its magnificent, voluminous interior. Standing beneath the dome you get an extraordinary sense of sculpted space, and of the serenity of its rigidly symmetrical plan. Ayasofya is the principal monograph of Byzantine architecture, which sought to create magical interiors from a mastery of the effects of light and shadow.

The exterior of the church is impressive only for its great size. Apart from the dome, its shape is lost behind additional buttresses and attractive Ottoman tombs, fountains, minarets and outbuildings. The massive fragments of classical columns, capitals and entablature which surround the entrance belong to the first two churches that stood here, built in the 4th and 5th centuries respectively. The original entrance to the church was through a vaulted courtyard.

The Narthex and the Vestibule of Warriors

The lobby, or narthex, is an impressive long chamber riveted in thin sheets of marble. The central bronze door into the body of the church guards the Imperial gate which was reserved for formal processions led by the emperor or patriarch. On the apex of the door a dove flies out of the Gospel of St John, opened at the 10th chapter and inscribed 'Our lord spoke, "I am the door of the sheep." ' Above is the celebrated mosaic of the Emperor Leo VI prostrate before Christ, flanked by medallions of the Virgin and the archangel Gabriel. It is believed to have been donated by Leo in 920 in repentance for his fourth, forbidden marriage, which caused the patriarch to refuse the emperor admittance through this very door.

At the south end of the narthex there is a curiously irregular, 6th-century entrance passage, known as the Vestibule of Warriors. This was as far as the armed bodyguard of the emperors was permitted to advance. Apart from the mosaic panel above the doorway, the

Mosaics inside Ayasofya

surviving patches of mosaic decoration date from the original church as well. The panel shows the Virgin and Christ receiving the homage of Justinian (left) and Constantine (right), who offer models of Ayasofya and the city in tribute. It dates from the 10th century.

The Nave

Justinian commissioned the greatest mathematician and the greatest physicist of his day, Anthemius of Tralles and Isidorus of Miletus, to build his new church and they came up with a dazzlingly innovative blueprint. Four massive piers, their lower courses bonded with lead, not mortar, support four great arches, which in turn support the circular base of a vast shallow dome, punctured by 40 windows. The great semidome apses to the east and west and load-bearing piers hidden in the structure of the lower side aisles give it the necessary support. The side aisles are but lightly separated from the central nave by columns which support an upper gallery and window-pierced upper walls.

The carved capitals which crown the columns are of bold Byzantine design. Their lace-like carving of vine leaves and foliate swirls surrounds Imperial monograms of Justinian and Theodora. They are undercut to make them all the more delicate, and to further belie their vital, load-bearing role. Look up at the outer face of the galleries which continue the play of light and dark with pearl and ebony inlays. The ceiling is still largely covered in gold mosaic decoration, believed to date from the 6th century. It is embellished with simple crosses and structural details are stressed by foliate and geometric borders.

The earliest figurative mosaic remaining in the church is that of the Virgin and Child in the eastern apse. It was unveiled in 867 and marked the triumph of Orthodoxy over the Iconoclastic movement which sought to banish images of the great Christian figures from church art. For all the majesty of her throne and supporting archangels (Gabriel to the right, Michael's feathers to the left) the

Ayasofya – symbol of Byzantine Constantinople

Virgin has a devastating sense of humanity. A young, frail and almost bewildered face stares out into the majestic prayer hall. High up on the northern wall, currently viewed through a forest of scaffolding, are three mosaic portraits: of St Ignatius the younger, St John Chrysostom and St Ignatius of Antioch.

Beneath the dome in each corner are the entwined wings of seraphim. The eastern pair are 14th-century mosaics whilst the western pair are painted copies. Their faces were covered by gilt medallions in the 19th century, when the Islamic roundels were hung from the upper gallery and the marble platforms for the muezzin, as well as the mihrab, minbar and sultan's personal prayer kiosk were installed. Notice that the floor of the apse has been slightly reorientated to face Mecca. In the south aisle Mahmut I built a delicate Koranic library, lined with Iznik tiles, in 1739.

Generations of Christians and Muslims have worn a deep hole through a brass plate and into the sweating column of St Gregory the Miracle Worker. Curiously moist to the touch, it is believed to cure eye disorders and to be a general aid to fertility.

The Upper Gallery and Mosaics

To admire the church's most impressive extant mosaics, negotiate the ramp from the narthex to the upper gallery, which was reserved for the women of Byzantium. The empress's throne was placed on the green marble roundel by the pair of free-standing green columns in the centre of the balcony. The walls were furnished with a glittering gallery of religious and historical mosaic portraits of which four have survived. The south wing of the gallery is divided in two by a marble screen carved to imitate a conventional wooden gate with keys, locks and decorative panels. Beyond it on the right is the magnificent 13th-century Deesis, an icon which traditionally showed Christ in Majesty with the Virgin and St John. The Virgin intercedes for us sinners from the left while St. John, our other great advocate, approaches Christ in judgement from the right.

At the far end of the southern gallery there are two groups of Imperial portraits. The oldest (mid 11th-century) depicts Christ Pantocrator flanked by the bejewelled figures of Zoë and her third husband Constantine IX Monomachus. Constantine's name and both their faces have been restored, for the mosaic originally depicted an earlier husband, and the Imperial pair were later disgraced and presumably erased for a period.

Separated from them by a window is a more elegant and realistic portrayal of John the Good and St Eirene with the Virgin and Child. John II Comnenus (1118–43) and the fair-headed, rosy-cheeked Eirene of Hungary are the most saintly and enlightened

Mosques and Mausoleums
A number of Muslim and Turkish architectural terms crop up in Istanbul. A mosque is a muslim prayer hall and will have at least one *minaret*, a free standing tower with a balcony – a *serefe* — from which the *muezzin* makes the call to prayer. Inside the mosque, on the south-southeast wall there will be a *mihrab*, a decorated arch which indicates the direction of Mecca towards which Muslims pray. To the right of the mihrab is a *minbar*, a pulpit-like staircase. A small prayer hall with neither a minbar, mihrab or minaret is known as a *mescit*. Near a mosque you will often find a *mektep*, a primary school run by the *hoça* and a courtyard *medrese*, a college for Koranic studies. Every mosque has a *sadirvan*, a fountain for ritual washing before prayers. This should not be confused with a *sebil*, a public fountain, often added to the outer wall of the more elaborate mosque complexes which are known as a *külliye*. A külliye will often contain a *türbe*, the mausoleum of a pious or Imperial founder, a *tabhane*, a lodging room for itinerant dervishes and a *tekke*, a dervish assembly room. It may also include an *imaret*, a public kitchen and a *hastane*, a hospital, which was supported by charges for the public bath or *hamam* and the *han*, an enclosed two-storey courtyard rented out to merchants and artisans.

pair to have occupied the Imperial throne. It is thought that the separate portrait of Prince Alexius, to their right, was commissioned after his early death in 1120.
In the north gallery there is one small mosaic tucked up in a dark corner on the east face of the northwest pier. It represents the Emperor Alexander gorgeously attired, holding an orb in one hand and a scroll in the other. He was a debauched, drunken, violent and near-pagan ruler, whose disastrous, 13-month reign was cut short when he suffered a stroke playing polo in the heat of the day after a heavy lunch.
Open: 09.30–17.00hrs; Upper Gallery 09.30–11.30, 13.00–16.00hrs. *Closed:* Monday. Admission charge. Photography charge.

◆
AYNALIKAVAK KASRI
Kasımpaşa, north shore of Golden Horn (Haliç)
This building was originally part of an early 18th-century palace set in favourite royal woods and vineyards. It was in the grand audience chamber here that the Treaty of Aynalıkavak was signed in 1784, ceding the Crimea to Russia. The rest of the 'Arsenal' palace (named after the nearby contemporary naval harbour) has disappeared. Nevertheless this many-windowed pavilion and its garden still reflect the tranquillity enjoyed here by the sultans. Its thoroughly restored 19th-century interior is open as

a museum, and the bottom floor is being converted into a 'Centre for Research into Turkish Music' and contains an eclectic display of instruments. *Open:* 09.30–16.00hrs. *Closed:* Monday and Thursday.

◆
BEŞIKTAŞ VAPUR ISKELESI (BEŞIKTAŞ LANDING)
European shore of lower Bosphorus (Boğaziçi)
Water-front gardens stretch either side of the Beşiktaş pier, with cafés and a few restaurants. The large ferries leave for Üsküdar between 06.00 and 23.45hrs every 20 minutes or for Kadıköy between 07.15 and 20.45hrs every half-hour. There is also a team of smaller ferries which get busy during the peak commuting hours. To catch the Bosphorus cruise walk 220 yards (200m) downstream to the Barbaros Hayreddin Vapur İskelesi (Hayrettin Paşa landing). Directly behind Beşiktaş landing is a monumental statue of Barbarossa, the great corsair admiral, and his tomb (which is equipped with a potted biography). Further inland, on the other side of the road, is an attractive covered vegetable and flower market and there are two cafés beside the brick and stone walls of the Sinan Paşa Mosque. It was built for Admiral Sinan who achieved his high rank by virtue of being the younger brother of Rüstem Paşa, the villainous Grand Vizier who, in alliance with Roxelana, dominated the last years of Süleyman the Magnificent's reign.

Commerce outside Beyazıt Mosque

◆◆◆
BEYAZIT CAMII
Beyazit Meydani, Eminönü
The mosque of Sultan Beyazit II is the oldest surviving great mosque in Istanbul. It was finished in 1506 by a virtually unknown architect, yet it ushers in the great classical age of Ottoman architecture. Beyazit Mosque has an atmosphere all of its own, for nowhere else does street life press quite so close and incessantly, to the actual doors of a great mosque. This gives the arcaded courtyard an exaggerated sense of serenity. It is a harmonious and dignified enclosure, equipped with a much-restored but charming domed washing fountain. The 20 assorted columns of granite, and green and red Egyptian porphyry are antique but were topped by Islamic capitals. The interior draws on Ayasofya

for inspiration with its central dome, flanked by a pair of semidomes, supported by four massive piers. Here however, the lower side aisles have been drawn into the great central space by double arches springing from a pair of stout granite columns. There is no gallery but a projecting pavilion on either side. This reclusive area seems redundant but may have been screened off for women or teaching.

The mosque's minarets have been inlaid with red stone, their bases decorated on alternate faces with a design of square Kufic script. By the northern minaret, just inside the book market, a gate leads into the enclosed garden and tomb of Sultan Beyazit, an attractive domed octagonal limestone building with details picked out in an inlay of green stone. The painted interior, with its landscape views, dates from a later restoration.

Beyazit Square – on the edge of the colourful market quarter

◆◆

BEYAZIT MEYDANI (BEYAZIT SQUARE)

Eminönü

This is one of the city's most fascinating public spaces, an irregular area just to the west of the Covered Bazaar, overlooked by the Moorish gateway of the University and the twin minarets of Beyazit Mosque. The pavements and walls glitter with the magpie-nest stalls of an open-air flea market. Nowhere else are you so clearly reminded of Istanbul's position as a natural market, for citizens from all over Istanbul and visitors alike search here, intent on a bargain. Mingled among the trails of shoppers are café chairs, sprawling along terraces, beside fountains and under the protecting shade of trees of idleness.

On the opposite side of Ordu Caddesi are some antique columns with a distinctive peacock-eye motif that were discovered in a road-widening process in the 1950s. They are

the remains of the Forum Tauri, one of the four great public squares of Byzantium, of which Beyazit Meydani is a direct successor. It was named Tauri after its central, hollow, bronze bull, used to roast notorious criminals such as the Emperor Phocas in 610. There are also some carved marble panels built into the lowest course of the ruins of Beyazit Hamam (at the roadside beyond the square), which once decorated the triumphal arch of Theodosius the Great (379–95).

◆◆

BEYLERBEY SARAYI (PALACE OF THE LORD OF LORDS)

Abdullah Ağa Caddesi, Beylerbey, Asiatic shore of the Bosphorus

Beylerbey is a late 19th-century sultan's palace almost directly beneath the first suspension bridge, Boğaziçi Köprüsü. The palace retains most of its original furnishings: a collection of Bohemian crystal, Persian carpets, French gilt furniture, Ming vases and Italian painted panels, which conjure up that century's opulent taste. In addition there are presents brought by visiting monarchs who often stayed here. It is the third Ottoman palace to have stood on this site and was designed as a summer house for Sultan Abdül Aziz (1861–76). It was built by Sarkis Balyan, the younger brother of Nikogos who had finished the Dolmabahçe Palace only 10 years before.

The long cobbled entrance tunnel, complete with music and discreetly lit displays of porcelain, leads into the secluded front garden of the palace where there are café tables from which to admire the tufa pool, the Rouillard lions, mature trees and immaculate box-trimmed flower beds. Two marble pavilions sheltered beneath bizarre multi-podded roofs look directly on to the Bosphorus.

Guides conduct tours through the palace which is divided between the semalik, the public rooms where male visitors could be received, and the harem where the sultan and his family lived. Look out for the admiral's sitting room, with its furniture of gilded wood, carved as rope, and the main reception room with its central marble pool and ceiling painted with panels of naval combat. The family dining room is equipped with inlaid chairs decorated with the *tuğra* (calligraphic monogram) of Abdül Hamit II, who was a skilled cabinet-maker himself. The two downstairs bedrooms were used by this sultan and his wife from 1913 to 1918, after a period of exile following his deposition in 1909. Upstairs is the principal room of the harem, an extraordinary blue marble and gilt reception room, its ceiling decorated with Ottoman poetry. Look out for the Ottoman clock in the side hall. The diamond and ruby hands come together to form the national symbol at noon, the hour of the midday prayer. Like all those in the palaces of Istanbul, the clock is stopped at 09.05hrs, the time of Atatürk's death.

Open: 09.00–12.00hrs, 13.30–17.00hrs. *Closed:* Monday and Thursday. Admission charge. Photography charge.

BLUE MOSQUE see **SULTANAHMET CAMII**

◆

BODRUM CAMII

Mesih Paşa Caddesi, off Laleli Caddesi, Eminönü

The exterior of the Bodrum Mosque hints at its Byzantine origins in the courses of slender brick and the small window-punctured dome. The double narthex (entrance hall), a nave divided into three by high narrow columns and a dome set over the transept confirm the impression. Final proof is provided by the mihrab which is offset slightly to point towards Mecca, out of alignment with the easterly apse.

The building was built by co-Emperor Romanus I Lecapenus at the start of the 10th century, adjoining his palace in what is now a scruffy public garden. This, like the old palace, is perched on top of a 5th-century cistern, supported by 75 columns. Theophano, his widow, turned the palace into the famous Myrelaion nunnery and was buried in the substantial crypt (sometimes referred to as the underground mosque).

This, as well as the cistern, is closed but can be glimpsed at from the stairs to the right of the minaret. The nunnery was converted into a mosque soon after the Turkish conquest, by Mesih Paşa, a Muslim convert from the Imperial Palaeologue dynasty.

◆◆◆

BOSPHORUS TRIP ✓

A cruise up the Bosphorus (Boğaziçi) should not be missed, however short your visit to Istanbul. Ferries leave from Eminönü and steam past the great palaces and mosques that line the lower Bosphorus, stopping only at Hayrettin Paşa for more passengers. They then glide up the wide channel of the upper Bosphorus, stopping at the five villages described below and passing many more. The handsome clapperboard mansions, known as *yalıs*, which decorate the shorelines present their only decorated face to the Bosphorus so little is missed by not venturing on land.

Kanlıca and Hidiv Kasrı

Asian shore

Kanlıca's principal attraction is its famous yoghurt, which is offered with jam, sugar or ice cream at the pier-side café. Hidiv Kasrı, an art-deco summer palace built by Abbas Hilmi, Khedive of Egypt in 1906. It remained occupied by his family until the 1930s but is now a hotel. For the price of a drink you can see the central fountain room, lined with mirrors, the bowed dining room, the Bosphorus terrace, and the curved art-deco lift to the tower. (See **Accommodation** if you fancy a room).

Yeniköy

European shore

Yeniköy means new town, a direct translation of the Byzantine resort of Neapolis that occupied this site. There are a

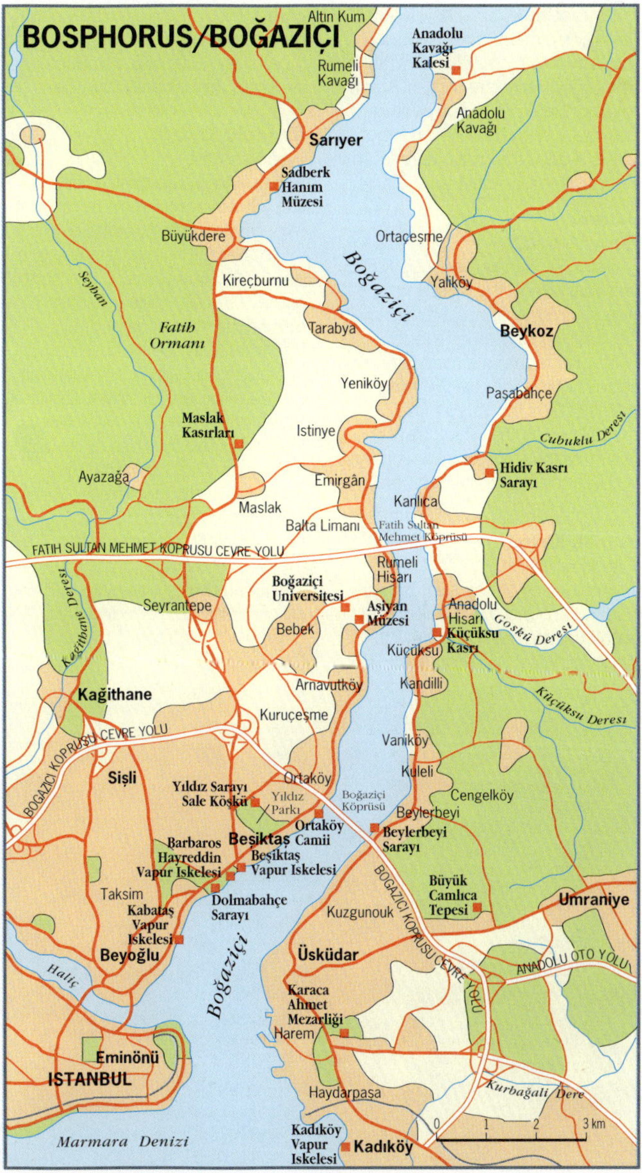
BOSPHORUS/BOĞAZIÇI
Altın Kum
Anadolu Kavağı Kalesi
Rumeli Kavağı
Anadolu Kavağı
Sarıyer
Sadberk Hanım Müzesi
Büyükdere
Ortaçeşme
Boğaziçi
Kireçburnu
Yaliköy
Seyban
Fatib Ormanı
Tarabya
Beykoz
Yeniköy
Pasabahçe
Maslak Kasırları
Istinye
Cubuklu Deresi
Hidiv Kasrı Sarayı
Ayazağa
Emirgân
Kanlıca
Maslak
Balta Limanı
Fatih Sultan Mehmet Köprüsü
FATIH SULTAN MEHMET KOPRUSU CEVRE YOLU
Rumeli Hisarı
Kağıthane Deresi
Boğaziçi Universitesi
Seyrantepe
Aşiyan Müzesi
Anadolu Hisarı
Gosku Deresi
Bebek
Küçüksu Kasrı
Küçüksu
Arnavutköy
Kandilli
Kağithane
Küçüksu Deresi
Kuruçeşme
BOGAZICI KOPRUSU CEVRE YOLU
Vaniköy
Kuleli
Sişli
Ortaköy
Cengelköy
Yıldız Sarayı Sale Köşkü
Yıldız Parkı
Boğaziçi Köprüsü
Beylerbeyi
Ortaköy Camii
Beylerbeyi Sarayı
Barbaros Hayreddin
Beşiktaş
Beşiktaş Vapur Iskelesi
Vapur Iskelesi
Büyük Camlıca Tepesi
Taksim
Dolmabahçe Sarayı
Umraniye
Kabataş Vapur Iskelesi
Kuzgunouk
BOGAZICI KOPRUSU CEVRE YOLU
Beyoğlu
Üsküdar
ANADOLU OTO YOLU
Haliç
Boğaziçi
Karaca Ahmet Mezarliği
Harem
Eminönü
ISTANBUL
Kurbağali Dere
Haydarpaşa
0
1
2
3 km
Kadıköy Vapur Iskelesi
Kadıköy
Marmara Denizi

couple of small fish restaurants and pier-borne cafés around the landing, from which small ferries cross to the larger Asian town of Beykoz. In the spring Emirgan, two miles (3km) south, hosts a colourful tulip festival in the gardens behind the village.

Sarıyer

European shore

This large village has a covered fish market on the shore which you should visit before taking a seat at one of the half-dozen restaurants that surround it. From here taxis run the nine miles (15km) to Kilyos for swimming in the Black Sea. A few hundred yards downstream is the excellent Sadberk Hanım Museum (see separate entry).

Rumeli Kavağı

European shore

A number of cheap restaurants cluster around the pier of this small fishing village. The grander establishments are along the corniche to the north but all serve, in season, the local speciality of Black Sea mussels, kebabs and sauce.

Anadolu Kavağı

Asian shore

At the end of the cruise the ferry halts here for an hour or two, giving enough time to walk up to the hilltop castle and eat in one of the cheap harbour-front cafés. The 'Genoese' castle above the village is actually Byzantine, as the fragments of carving and Greek inscriptions on the two central towers and outer curtain wall reveal. It was known as the fortress of Heiron and served as the naval and customs headquarters for the Bosphorus. It is in a superb position with a clear view out to the Black Sea and in pre-Christian times a temple to Zeus stood here, surrounded by a courtyard dedicated to the 12 Olympian deities.

◆◆

BOZDOĞAN KEMERI (VALENS' AQUEDUCT)

Arches across border of Fatih and Eminönü

This imposing double line of arches astride an urban valley is not so much a site to be visited as a passing feature that flicks in and out of view. This may change as work progresses on the planned promenade along its summit. The aqueduct was built at the end of the 4th century by the Emperor Valens to connect Istanbul's third and fourth hills and so bring clean water from the Belgrade forest to a distribution point above the Forum Tauri, modern Beyazit Square. It was still in full working order less than a hundred years ago.

Rumeli Kavağı was a principal toll and control point on the upper Bosphorus in Byzantine times

◆

BULGAR KILISE (ST STEPHEN OF THE BULGARS)

Vapur Iskelesi Caddesi, Fatih

On the parkland shore of the Golden Horn (Haliç) stands this completely cast-iron church. An ornate curiosity, it was cast in Vienna and assembled here in 1871 when the Bulgarian Orthodox church broke away from the authority of the Greek patriarch of Constantinople. Within the railings you can see the tombs of the first Bulgarian patriarchs.

◆

CAFERAĞA MEDRESE

Caferiye Sokağı, Eminönü

A bust of the great architect Sinan overlooks this small and rather sparse courtyard he designed. Built as a Koranic college in 1559, it was commissioned by Cafer Ağa, the chief black eunuch under Süleyman the Magnificent. The students' cells are now occupied by artisans demonstrating ceramic, paper marbling and other skills round a cluster of café tables in the centre.

◆◆

ÇEMBERLITAŞ (CONSTANTINE'S COLUMN)

Divan Yolu Caddesi, Eminönü

Blackened, riveted, patched both above and below, this great porphyry column with its laurel wreath bands stands as a totem of the city's enduring vivacity. It was erected by Constantine the Great as part of the dedication of his new city on 11 May 330, at the centre of the arcaded oval Forum of Constantine. Holy relics rescued by Aeneas from the sack of Troy in 1180BC still lie embedded in its base. Now about 115 feet (35m) high, it originally topped 165 feet (50m) with its Corinthian capital and gorgeous gilded statue of the emperor in the attributes of Apollo. This was dislodged by lightning in 1105 and replaced with a cross, which was removed by Mehmet II after the conquest of 1453. The metal hoops and messy base were added in 1779 after a fire devastated the Covered Bazaar and blackened the column.

CHORA see **KARIYE CAMII**

COVERED BAZAAR/MARKET see **KAPALIÇARŞI**

◆

DENIZ MÜZESI (MARITIME MUSEUM)

119 Dolmabahçe Caddesi, by Beşiktaş Vapur Iskelesi (Landing)

The Maritime Museum is surrounded by an open-air display of ships' cannon and will appeal to enthusiasts of ephemera and Ottoman history. A dragon-shaped cannon captured from Vienna in 1683, the 16th-century armour worn by the last Mameluke Sultan of Egypt, glass grenades and Barbarossa's standard can be found among the extensive collection of model ships, naval uniforms, weapons and portraits in the main hall. A second gallery, with its collection of caiques and Imperial barges, is of more general interest.

Open: 09.30–12.30hrs, 13.30–17.00hrs. *Closed:* Monday and Tuesday.

◆

DOLMABAHÇE CAMII

On Meclisi Mebusan Caddesi, 330 yards (300m) upstream from Kabataş Vapur Iskelesi (Landing)

The Dolmabahçe Mosque is a conspicuous feature of the Bosphorus shoreline with its pair of tapering minarets and its high single dome. It was built conveniently close to the new palace in 1853 by Nikoğos Balyan for Valide Bezmialem, the mother of the reigning Sultan Abdül Mecit. The landward entrance presents an ordered Renaissance façade but warning of the rococo is given by the slender soaring minarets, in the form of Corinthian columns whose capitals give flower to a balcony and needle lantern. The interior is like a ballroom offered to God with its exuberant painted dome, window panels and squinches. The high prayer hall is well lit by great windows which pierce the three outer walls overlooking the Bosphorus. Indeed the quality of the interior light is almost enough to excuse the decorative excess of the dome's exterior, which can be admired from the tea house in the mid 18th-century tomb opposite.

◆◆

DOLMABAHÇE SARAYI

Entrance by the clock tower on Dolmabahçe Caddesi, midway between Kabataş and Beşiktaş Landings

This vast mid-19th-century palace, home of the Ottoman

Dolmabahçe Palace

sultans from 1853 to 1922, is at its best from the outside, looking exuberant and imperious from a passing Bosphorus boat. Its gardens are formally impressive, but the hurried tours through the interior, though unforgettable, can happily be missed by those who dislike excessive grandeur and decoration. Built for Abdül Mecit by Nikoğos Balyan, the entire central section of the palace is an absurdly large state hall, which is more theatrical than imperial and despite its vast scale fails to impress. Among the huge quantities of carpets, chandeliers, magnificent *scagliola* (composite marble) columns, gilded clocks and pots are an enviable alabaster bathroom and a staircase with crystal banisters. Despite its slight charms the palace remains extremely popular – go early to be sure of securing one of the daily allocation of tickets.
Open: 09.00–17.00hrs. *Closed:* Monday and Thursday. Admission charge. Photography charge.

◆◆

EYÜP

West bank of the Golden Horn (Haliç)
Eyüp is named after Eyüp Ensari, the standard bearer and Companion of the Prophet Mohammed, buried here after he died directing the unsuccessful Arab siege of the city (674–678). The Byzantines agreed to respect his tomb and it survived eight centuries of Christianity to be conveniently 'rediscovered' during the Turkish siege. Eyüp proved to be a great morale booster and after the final victorious assault he was adopted as the patron saint of the Ottoman dynasty. Mehmet II enlarged the tomb, adding a great mosque and various charitable outbuildings. It quickly developed into a pilgrimage centre and a propitious place to be buried, and was forbidden to unbelievers. Eyüp was also firmly established in the ritual life of the Empire. Each successor had to ride out of the city on a white horse to Eyüp's tomb where the sheikh of the local dervishes 'crowned' the new sultan by kissing his left shoulder and girding him with the sabre of Osman.
Mehmet II's buildings were destroyed in the 1766 earthquake and the present sanctuary was completed in 1800. In the broad outer courtyard, shaded by poplars, a fountain plays and children scamper amongst the flocks of well-fed pigeons. Baroque gateways guard the entrance to the inner court in which the off-centre tomb is surrounded by a high and formal colonnade. Eyüp's mausoleum is covered inside and out with rich Iznik and Kütahya tiles. The well-polished pilgrim window was added by Ahmet I. Opposite is the richly painted and gilded interior of the mosque.
A rewarding excursion from here is to walk uphill through the enormous Turkish cemetery to reach the Pierre Loti Teahouse which enjoys a

The Koran in the mosque at Eyüp

tranquil view over the Golden Horn. It is named after the diminutive French naval officer who haunted the cafés of Eyüp during his secretive affair with a lady from a harem. This tragic love affair was the background for Loti's celebrated Orientalist novel, *Aziyade*.

◆◆

FATIH CAMII (SULTAN MEHMET FATIH CAMII)

Fevzi Paşa Caddesi, Fatih

The baroque mosque of the Conqueror is the third great religious building to crown the fourth hill of Istanbul.
Constantine the Great built the Church of the Holy Apostles here at the beginning of the 4th century, the chosen burial place of the emperors for 800 years. It survived until the conquest, when it was symbolically used as a quarry for the great mosque that Mehmet the Conqueror raised here between 1463 and 1470. This was destroyed by an earthquake in the mid-18th century and Mustafa III immediately employed his talented architect Mehmet Tahir Ağa to create an entirely new mosque. The spacious elevated terrace surrounded by schools, colleges and charitable institutions also dates from this period.
The exterior of the Fatih Mosque presents an ordered cascade of leaded domes enlivened by the exaggerated cornices of the 18th century. The square prayer hall is expansive and dignified, with stencilled decoration on the soaring domes. The side galleries and the sultan's lodge are used as a school for Imams which accounts for the noticeably devout tone of the precincts. Do not however be put off from refreshing yourself from the pump-action fountain in the corner. The outer and inner gates of the courtyard are

of a different stone, as these tall, narrow arches hung with 'stalactites' survive from the 15th-century mosque. So too does the charming central fountain whose roof, an overhanging conical hat, is shaded by cedar trees. Even rarer survivors are the tiled lunettes on the two windows in the west wall. This striking swirl of yellow, blue and white is an example of early Iznik work using the *cuerda seca* technique where the fields of colour were kept apart by thin lines of grease which emerge black from the firing.

The marble hexagonal mausoleum of Mehmet II and the simpler tomb of his wife Gülbahar lie to the east of the mosque. The enormous embroidered tomb capped with a large turban is seldom found without at least one respectful Turk circling it with prayers.

Tomb open: 10.00–16.30hrs. *Closed:* Monday and Tuesday.

Ritual washing at Fatih Mosque

◆

FENARI ISA CAMII (THE MOSQUE OF CONSTANTINE LIPS)

North side of Adnan Menderes (Vatan) Caddesi, Fatih

The monastic church of Theotokos Panochratis (the Immaculate Mother of God) was founded by Constantine Lips, a 10th-century courtier, and re-established by the Empress Theodora after the 13th-century Byzantine reconquest. She built another church on the southern wall and later added a mortuary chapel, hence creating a triple-naved church. As it was then customary to divide the altar of a church into three apses, this created an extraordinary undulating eastern façade, whose exterior ripples across seven apses. The friezes on this wall are a virtuoso demonstration of the bricklayer's art. The swirls, inversions, herring bone, zigzag and interlinked swastika patterns draw freely upon the ancient designs of Mesopotamia and Lycia. The interior has been sympathetically restored to expose many of the original features – the powerful barrel vaulting, carved capitals and cornices – while remaining a working prayer hall. It was renamed Fenari Isa, the Lamp

of Jesus, when it was first converted in 1496 for use by a Sufi community. The roof has curious tunnel-like buttresses round the southern dome, which were tiny rooftop chapels.
Open: hours of prayer.

◆
FETHIYE CAMII (THE CHURCH OF THEOTOKOS PAMMAKARISTOS)
Fethiye Caddesi, Fatih
The Byzantine Church of the Joyous Mother of God served as the patriarchate of Constantinople for over a hundred years after the Muslim conquest of the city. It was converted into a mosque and renamed Fethiye (Victory) by Murat III to celebrate his conquest of the mountainous kingdoms of the Caucasus, Georgia and Azerbaijan, in 1591.
The intriguing brickwork exterior conceals a chapel on the southern side, decorated with some magnificent frescos which were commissioned by Maria, the widow of General Tarchionates, at the beginning of the 14th century. The chapel has a separate entrance, but it is no longer open on a regular basis, though the Director of the Archaeological Institute can give permission for visits.
Open: hours of prayer.

◆
GALATA KÖPRÜSÜ (GALATA BRIDGE)
Over the Golden Horn (Haliç)
The new Galata Bridge, completed in 1992, is the fifth to have spanned this reach of the Golden Horn since the first wooden one was constructed in 1845. It is a technical improvement on the extant old bridge whose pontoons do much to prevent the movement of fresh water into the Golden Horn. Two drawbridges open to allow shipping to pass. There is still hope that the alley of seedy bars and restaurants of the old bridge will be allowed back one day.

◆
GALATA KULESI (GALATA TOWER)
Galip Dede Caddesi, Karaköy
The Galata Tower was built in 1348 as the apex of the Genoese defences. It is the most distinctive building in Karaköy, and emerges clear of the roofline with its restored 19th-century conical hat. At 203 feet (62m) it served as a fire watchtower throughout the Ottoman period but in the 1960s it was converted into a tourist attraction. The interior is now entirely modern and quite tacky, though the view from the top-floor balcony at dusk compensates.
Open: 09.00–22.00hrs (restaurant-nightclub open 20.00–24.00hrs). Admission charge (allows use of the lift).

◆
GÜLHANE PARK
Alemdar Caddesi, Eminönü
This wooded public park was created from the old rose garden, the *gül hane*, on the lower terrace of the Topkapı Palace. Immediately to the left of the entrance look out for the Alay Köşkü, one of the eyes of the sultan. It perches up a ramp on a corner of the walls and was

used by the sultans to watch events at the gatehouse and offices of the Grand Vizier, which were immediately below. The central promenade of the park leads past a number of cafés and a sad zoo on the left, complete with caged cats, rabbits, dogs and chickens among greater exotica. On the right up by the old slag-decorated cascade is an aquarium housed in an old Roman cistern and beyond it a dilapidated Tanzimat museum, commemorating the early 19th-century reform movement.

At the far end of the park, below the back gate to Topkapı Palace, is a remarkably well-preserved 3rd-century victory monument surrounded by clapperboard teahouses. It is known as the Column of the Goths and the inscription on its base reads 'to Fortune, who returns by reason of the victory over the Goths'.

Seraglio Point beyond is ornamented with a statue of Kemal Atatürk and has a superb view of the Bosphorus. To the west a 17th-century Imperial boathouse, the Sepetçiler Köşkü, has been restored as a Press Centre, and the bar, café and seafront garden are thoughtfully left open to the public.

◆

HAGHIOS GEORGIOS (ST GEORGE)

Near Sadrazam Ali Paşa Caddesi, Fatih

The Church of St George has been the headquarters of the Greek Orthodox Patriarch of Constantinople since 1601. It was entirely rebuilt in 1720 to a simple basilica plan as the Christian minorities of the Ottoman Empire were forbidden domes. Three aisles lead to a massive wooden iconostasis with the famous pair of portable mosaics on the extreme right. In one, the formal gold and red toga of the Christ child contrasts strongly with the mournful flesh tones of the Virgin Mary. The other shows St John the Baptist on a gold background with the donors in medallions top and bottom left. Beside them on the south wall are three reliquaries containing the bones of St Omonia, St Theophano and St Euphemia. Another great treasure is the patriarchal throne inlaid with marble and mother-of-pearl double-headed eagles and carnations. The central gate was closed forever in protest at the lynching of Gregory V here in 1821.

Open: hours of prayer and at the discretion of the custodians.

◆

HAREM FERIBOT ISKELE

Asian shore of the lower Bosphorus (Boğaziçi)

Selimiye Kişlasi (Selimiye Barracks)

The vast quad of the Selimiye Barracks is the most distinctive building on the Asian shore. It was begun by Mahmut II in the early 19th century to house his new paid army after the destruction of the mutinous slave corps, the Janissaries. The three other wings were finished by his son Abdül Mecit just in time to be converted into a hospital by Florence

Nightingale during the Crimean War. Her rooms in the northeast tower are maintained as a museum.
Open: 09.00–17.00hrs on Saturday, other days by appointment, tel: 343 7310.

Selimiye Camii (Selimiye Mosque)
This elegant baroque mosque was built by Selim III just north of the later barracks. Great wheel-like arches support the drum that carries the single dome. The sombre prayer hall of grey marble almost equals the dignity of the exterior, and much of the original decoration remains: a pair of handsome brass candlesticks beside the mihrab and the finely stencilled pendentives and dome.

Crimean War Cemetery
This scrupulously maintained, secretive British commonwealth cemetery is down a drive off the highway south of the distinctive university buildings on Tibbiye Caddesi. Look out for a battered blue sign 'Commonwealth Harp Mezarligi Haydar Pasha'.
The Crimean war graves cluster below Queen Victoria's memorial, a striking sword-obelisk guarded by pre-Raphaelite angels and inscribed in four languages. The rest of the garden contains the graves of commonwealth citizens of other eras: near by is the 16th-century tombstone of Edward Barton, Queen Elizabeth I's ambassador who died whilst campaigning with Sultan Mehmet III against the Hungarians. The terrace continues past the Ionic temple

Ceramics – a centuries-old tradition

tomb of Nicholas O'Connor, through a flower garden to commemorate the many Muslim soldiers of the British Indian army who died in World War I.

Karaca Ahmet Mezarlig (Cemetery of Karaca Ahmet)
The dark green haze that frames the hills above Üsküdar and Kadiköy is created by the cypresses which grow amongst these four centuries of carved marble tombs. Karaca Ahmet cemetery is named after a famous 14th-century *gazi*, a swashbuckling Muslim knight, whose tomb was discovered here and embellished after the Turkish conquest. If you like romantic decay, fields of odd-angled, overgrown tombs and the calming melancholy of necropoli, you will love Karaca Ahmet, the largest cemetery of the Ottoman Empire.

HIPPODROME see **AT MEYDANI**

◆◆
HIRKA-I ŞERIF CAMII
Keçeciler Caddesi, Fatih
The Mosque of the Holy Mantle was built in 1851 by Sultan Abdül Mecit I to house the Prophet Mohammed's cloak. Two gateways give access to the high garden terrace that surrounds the mosque. It has an elegant Renaissance front, its principal entrance flanked by a pair of recessed bays, supported by Ionic columns. The pair of tapering minarets are Corinthian columns whose capitals bud into balconies. The octagonal prayer hall is enclosed by outer galleries, like an ornate jewel held by protective clasps. It is exuberantly decorated with fine marble furnishings, a magnificent entablature and calligraphic frieze. The holy mantle is secure in a small octagonal sanctuary behind the mihrab arch.
Open: hours of prayer.

◆◆
IMRAHOR CAMII (ST JOHN OF STUDION)
Imam Asir Sokağı, Imrahor Ilyas Caddesi, Fatih
Istanbul's oldest church, from the 5th century, is tucked away in the southwestern corner of the city. For a thousand years it was one of the spiritual nerve centres of Byzantium, but is now quite awkward to find and more than half ruined. Look out for a crumbling brick minaret, added in the 16th century, which serves as a useful marker for the entrance gate. A squatter family lives among the ruins and makes a small living collecting tips.
The Church of St John was built in 463 and named after its patron, the Consul Studius. It was run by an Akoimati community which used shifts of monks to keep a perpetual vigil of prayer. The monastery survived the conquest long enough to celebrate its millenium, but was then converted into a mosque by the cavalry general, or İmrahor, of Sultan Beyazit II. Until a shattering earthquake in 1894 the mosque remained essentially intact. The four Corinthian capitals of the narthex or entrance portal, drilled not carved, hint at the lace-like capitals of Byzantium that would soon be produced. The nave, like most early Byzantine churches, looks back to the plan of the Roman law courts. It is divided into three aisles by rows of green marble columns, one of which still stands supporting its original carved entablature. The floor is paved in the colourful geometrical swirls of marble mosaic.

◆
ISTIKLÂL CADDESI
Beyoğlu
The old Grande Rue de Péra, is a pedestrian avenue that runs from Taksim Meydani through the heart of Beyoğlu. It is one of the primary shopping streets of Istanbul, intersected by numerous side streets lined with seedy bars, nightclubs, restaurants and churches. The major architectural interest

comes from the old embassy buildings, which became consulates when Ankara became capital of Turkey. The first embassy building from Taksim Square is the white classical façade of the French consulate, near the Armenian church tucked up Zarback Sokaği. Half way down the street, Galatasaray School hides behind vast wrought iron gates, and the imposing British consulate is down Mesrutiyet Caddesi opposite. The most striking building, except perhaps for the brand new shop, Vakko, owned by the man who paid for the pedestrianisation, is a five-storey Venetian façade through which you pass to reach the Catholic church of St Anthony of Padua. Further down on the left is the pretty Dutch consulate with its prominent heraldic device of a gold lion on blue. Pertaçilar Sokak, next left, leads to a Protestant and a Catholic chapel. The former Soviet Union embassy, white pilasters against a red background, is behind the security screen at no 443.

◆

KADIKÖY VAPUR ISKELESI

The shore around the Kadiköy landing is a fish market. Boats bob by the harbour wall and the quay is lined with panniers overflowing with the glistening harvest of the Sea of Marmara (Marmara Denizi) and the Black Sea. To the north, the umbrellas of shore-front cafés stretch towards Haydarpaşa Station while a pleasant coastal park has been created to the south.

◆◆

KALENDERHANE CAMII (THEOTOKOS KYRIOTISSA)

16 Mart Sehitleri Caddesi, Eminönü

This handsome brick-built mosque is tucked beneath the east end of Bozdoğan Kemeri (Valens' Aqueduct). It was once the Byzantine church of Theotokos Kyriotissa, 'Her Ladyship Mary, the Mother of God' and was converted in the immediate aftermath of the Turkish conquest in 1453. Its name derives from the Kalender Sufi brotherhood, who used it as their monastery. Kalenderhane has been elegantly restored by a joint

Fishing boats on the Golden Horn

American/ Turkish team. The double narthex – the twin entrance hall – still carries fragments of Christian frescos. The prayer hall has an expansive cruciform plan, emphasised by wide barrel vaults that meet at the ribbed dome. Among the splendour of the marble walls, notice some original Byzantine capitals and cornices.

Now take a deep breath and remember that you are in Istanbul. Theotokos Kyriotissa was built in the 12th century, incorporating parts of a ruined 8th-century church that was itself a rebuilding of a 6th-century chapel, constructed from a Roman bath. A side chapel contains the city's unique pre-iconoclastic figurative mosaic and the only surviving frescos from the Latin occupation in the 13th century. The bad news is that it is firmly locked and under the control of the Antiquities Commission.

Open: hours of prayer.

◆

KANLI KILISE (ST MARY OF THE MONGOLS)

Merdivenli Mektep, off Sancaktar Yokusu, off Vodina Caddesi, Fatih

The name and history of this small, reclusive Greek Orthodox church are more interesting than the building itself. It was founded in 1282 by Princess Maria Palaelogina, who had returned to the city of her birth after an eventful 15-year marriage to the Mongol Great Khan Abagu. She refused to contemplate a second marriage and settled down here as a nun.

◆◆◆

KAPALIÇARŞI ✓ (COVERED BAZAAR)

Eminönü

This indoor labyrinth of over 4,000 shops is one of the world's most celebrated markets. Its plan is still substantially the same as when it was established in the 15th century, but it has been rebuilt several times after fires, most recently in the 1950s. Today it presents a rather sanitised version of its former self, but the shop-lined streets and alleyways are still irresistibly alluring.

At the very centre of the market is the Old Bedesten (Iç Bedesten), the only part of Mehmet the Conqueror's building left. Then, as now, it housed stalls selling the most valuable wares, for it can be locked extra securely at night. Elsewhere in the market, the traders tend to group according to their wares though this is by no means always true. There are knots of carpet dealers on Haliçilar Caddesi and clusters of jewellers on Kalpakçilar Caddesi for example. Otherwise, shopping here should be simply a matter of following your nose. There are restaurants, cafés and toilets in the Bazaar; shop-keepers will direct you.

Round the Covered Bazaar

Though the Covered Bazaar is a finite entity, the market itself spills out all round it into the neighbouring streets.

Hidden behind these streets is a whole series of courtyards

Glittering wares in the Covered Bazaar

known as *hans*, where, in former times, merchants from out of town would unload their goods, stable their pack animals and stay themselves, side by side with small workshops. These are now entirely devoted to manufacturing. **Valide Han**, for example, pulses to the rhythmic clack and shunt of thousands of looms, while in **Iç Cebeci Han** leather dyeing still goes on. Ask the shopkeepers to point these out to you as most of the entrances are very well camouflaged.

◆

KARA AHMET PAŞA CAMII

Topkapı Caddesi, near Topkapı Gate in Theodosian walls

This elegant little mosque was built by Sinan in the middle of the 16th century for one of Suleyman the Magnificent's Grand Viziers. Its spacious tree-shaded courtyard is surrounded by a colonnade which joins the mosque porch to a domed *medrese*, a Koranic college. The prayer hall is a supremely disciplined space. The central dome is supported by six semidomes carried by the arches that span the six free-standing columns. The *mihrab* niche is small but perfectly in proportion to the hall. Above the windows are panels of early calligraphic Iznik tiles in green, yellow and blue. These rare examples can also be seen above the porch windows.

Open: hours of prayer.

◆◆◆ KARIYE CAMII (CHORA) ✓

Kariye Camii Sokak, Fatih

Within this charming, rotund, pink Byzantine church glitters a treasure trove of dozens of late Byzantine mosaics and frescos, one of the most astonishing of Istanbul's sites. Quite apart from being the only group of this size in the city, they are among the most brilliant of their kind anywhere in the world. The religious subject matter, from the lives of the Virgin and Christ, is treated with such an earthly vitality that the images demand belief in their historical reality. Yet at the same time the works are imbued with a wondrous and gentle spirituality.

The church of St Saviour in Chora, which means in the country, was originally a monastic church built beyond the Constantinian city walls. The current building dates from between the 11th and 14th centuries while the mosaics were all executed between 1315 and 1321. They were commissioned and overseen by Grand Logothete Theodore Metochites, the controller of the state treasury, whose resplendent yet humble portrait, offering the church to Christ, can be seen over the entrance to the nave from the inner narthex. Though converted into a mosque in the early 16th century, most of the mosaics and paintings survived to be restored in the middle of

KARIYE CAMII

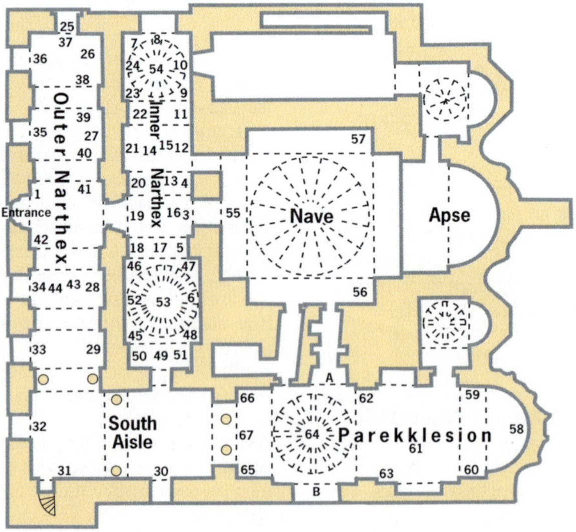

this century by the Byzantine Institute of America.

At first the church seems an indecipherable mass of gilded images, but these do break down into three main series. In the outer narthex, and spilling round the right-hand dome of the inner narthex, is the cycle showing Christ's life and work (25–54). Events from the life of the Virgin (7–24) occupy the rest of the inner narthex, except the interior of the domes themselves which depict the ancestors of Christ. There are three further mosaics in the marble-clad nave (55–7).

The side chapel to the right, known as the Parekklesion, was originally used as a burial place with tombs in the four now empty niches. The frescos which decorate it reflect this with their depiction of the Christian iconography of death. The painting in the semidome of the apse shows the Harrowing of Heaven and Hell (58), with Christ pulling Adam and Eve from their tombs so that they can accompany him into Heaven. It is one of the world's finest frescos. The dedicatory mosaics (1, 2, 3 and 6) are all of a luminous spiritual quality.

Key to Plan of Mosaics and Paintings

Dedicatory Mosaics

1 Virgin with angels
2 Christ Pantocrator
3 The donor presents the Church to Christ
4 St Peter
5 St Paul
6 Christ and the Virgin with two earlier donors, Isaac Comnenus and Mari Melane

The Life of the Virgin

7 Rejection of Joachim's (the Virgin's father) offerings
8 Joachim
9 Joachim
10 The Annunciation to St Anne
11 The meeting of Joachim and Anne
12 The birth of the Virgin
13 The Virgin's first seven steps
14 The priests' blessing
15 The Virgin caressed by her parents
16 The Virgin's presentation in the Temple
17 The Virgin is fed bread by the angels
18 The instruction of the Virgin in the temple
19 The Virgin is given a skein of purple wool
20 Zacharias prays to God to help him find a husband for Mary
21 Joseph's rod sprouts leaves and Mary is betrothed to him
22 Joseph escorts Mary home
23 The Annunciation
24 Joseph leaves on business

The Life and Works of Christ

25 Joseph dreaming
26 The enrolment for taxation
27 The Nativity
28 The Journey of the Three Wise Men
29 Herod consults the priests and scribes
30 The flight into Egypt
31 The Massacre of the Innocents
32 The Massacre of the Innocents (cont)
33 Grieving mothers
34 The flight of Elizabeth and John the Baptist
35 The return from Egypt
36 Christ goes to Jerusalem for Passover
37 Christ among the priests in the temple

38 Christ with John the Baptist
39 Christ with John the Baptist
40 The temptation of Christ
41 The marriage feast at Cana
42 The miracle of the loaves
43 Christ healing a leper
44 Christ walking on the water (waves only)
45 Christ healing the blind and the dumb
46 Christ healing two blind men
47 Christ healing Peter's mother-in-law
48 Christ healing the woman with the issue of blood
49 Christ healing the man with the withered hand
50 Christ healing a leper
51 An unidentified healing scene
52 Christ healing the sick
53 Christ surrounded by ancestors
54 Christ and the Virgin surrounded by ancestors
55 The dormition of the Virgin
56 The Virgin Mary
57 Christ

Byzantine treasures in Kariye Camii

The Parekklesion

58 The harrowing of heaven and hell
59 Christ raising the widow's son
60 Christ raising Jairus' daughter
61 The Second Coming of Christ and Last Judgement
62 Moses and the burning bush
63 The dedication of the Temple of Solomon
64 The Virgin and Child with angels
65 Isaiah and the angel
66 Aaron and his sons in front of the altar
67 The souls of the righteous in God's hand

The Tombs

A Theodore Metochites
B Michael Tomikes, general and friend of Metochites

Open: 09.00–16.30hrs. *Closed:* Tuesday. Bus: 87 from Taksim to Edirnekapı

◆

KILIÇ ALI PAŞA CAMII AND THE TOPHANE

Necatibey Caddesi, Beyoğlu

In 1580 Ali, the governor of Algiers, Admiral in Chief of the Ottoman navy and the conqueror of Tunis, retired to Istanbul. He commissioned the court architect, Sinan, to build a mosque and asked the sultan where it should rise. Murat III replied, half in jest, half in wisdom, 'in the Admirals' domain, the sea'. Ali Paşa promptly filled in part of the Bosphorus shore and erected his mosque, tomb and associated charitable buildings there.

Sinan designed the mosque's interior as a scaled-down replica of Ayasofya, but lost its magic in the process. The interior is sturdy and heavy, though it has been furnished with some vigorous blue and red calligraphic Iznik tiles. The lead clad roof is a further triumph of Sinan the cautious engineer over Sinan the experimental artist.

The porch is more successful and original and the ablution courtyard has an elegant fountain and an arcaded row of washtaps. Behind the mosque the admiral's hexagonal tomb is flanked by the main teaching chamber of the *medrese*. The large, black, dilapidated dome contains the hall of the original, still-functioning baths.

The Tophane

On the other side of the mosque, just beyond the precinct wall, is the Tophane Fountain, one of the half-dozen of the city's more elegant baroque fountains, named after the Tophane, the imperial cannon foundry, on the terrace above the road. The foundry dates from immediately after the conquest by Mehmet II but its bulky brick and stone building has been constantly remodelled. The lower terraces are embellished by the odd cannon, but the rest is still occupied by the military.

◆

KILISE CAMII

Tirendaz Sokak off Vefa Caddesi, Eminönü

The 14th-century Byzantine church of St Theodore was converted into Kilise Camii, the Church Mosque, immediately after the conquest in 1453. Fortunately little has been altered since then. Its dusty but elegant façade of columns and niches introduces a typical double entrance hall, or narthex. The right-hand dome in the narthex retains a small mosaic Christ medallion surrounded by eight figures neatly framed in geometrical borders.

Open: hours of prayer.

◆

KIZ TAŞI (MARCIAN'S COLUMN)

Kiztaşi Caddesi, Fatih

Take a snack at the Kiztaşi Lokantasi as a reward for finding this early Byzantine antiquity. A statue of the seated Emperor Marcian, who ruled from 450 to 457, once perched on its pediment with the four corner eagles at his feet. The granite column is now riveted in iron but stands on its original base.

The best preserved face shows a pair of winged Victories holding a medallion and the remains of the dedicatory script.

◆

KOCA MUSTAFA PAŞA CAMII

Koca Mustafa Paşa Caddesi, Fatih

This holy complex, a mosque, mausoleums, an old monastery and a hamam, form the central square of this quarter of the city. It was named after the Grand Vizier who converted the old Byzantine church of St Andrew here into a mosque at the beginning of the 16th century. He added the five-domed porch to the north face of the church and reorientated the interior to fit the Muslim direction of prayer. The interior has recently been painted a distressing shade of green but many of the Byzantine features still exist. The altar is on the left as you enter, a pair of elegant Byzantine capitals stand in the central nave overlooked by the original dome and there are some pale columns in the narthex.

Beside the minaret you can still see the 16th-century courtyard of a dervish monastery. The tombs of the dervish sheikhs are still venerated here, particularly that of the first Sheikh, Sümbül (Hyacinth) Efendi and his daughter Rahine who were once virtual patron saints of Istanbul. Rahine is buried in an open-air tomb, protected by a grilled screen surrounded, suitably, by hyacinths, and adjacent to the dead but still sacred tree.

◆◆

KÜÇÜK AYASOFYA CAMII (SS SERGIUS AND BACCHUS CHURCH)

Mehmet Paşa Sokak, Eminönü

This Byzantine church is one of Istanbul's most extraordinary and beautiful survivors, built a few years before Ayasofya, in AD 527. It has been in use as a mosque since the 16th century, but not even the five-domed entrance porch, minaret and courtyard *medrese* can disguise its tell-tale red brick exterior and stubby, undulating Byzantine dome. Once inside, there is a neglected, musty dampness, but the charming vitality of the building and its aura of great age triumph. Sergius and Bacchus were Roman soldiers martyred for their faith who became the patron saints of Christian soldiers. They had also saved Justinian from execution by appearing in a dream to his uncle Justin I and professing him innocent of plotting for the throne. As soon as Justinian came to the Imperial throne in 527, he built this church in their honour, with walls of marble and ceilings of mosaics. It was, according to Procopius, 'more resplendent than the sun, and everywhere was filled profusely with gold'.

Today the plain whitewashed interior allows visitors to concentrate on the building's extraordinary design, based on an off-centre octagon in an irregular rectangle. The octagonal nave is separated from two storeys of encircling aisles by pillars of alternating red and green marble. On the

ground floor these pillars are topped by bravely fanning capitals of exquisite lacework carving, a few still bearing the monogram of Justinian and Theodora. The roof, leading into a dome with 16 facets, is supported by arches growing out of the capitals of the first-floor pillars. Between the floors runs an encircling Greek inscription honouring Justinian, Theodora and Sergius, but mysteriously not Bacchus.
Open: hours of prayer. If not, ask any local to find the guardian.

◆◆
KÜÇÜKSU KASRI (KÜÇÜKSU PALACE)

Asian shore of lower Bosphorus, 550 yards (500m) downstream from Anadolu Hisarı
The exquisite icing sugar rococo palace of Küçüksu was built in 1857. Set in the meadow formed by the two streams which made up the Sweet Waters of Asia, a fashionable destination for Ottoman picnics, it is still in a marvellous position on the Bosphorus. It was built as a country cottage for Sultan Abdül Mecit I to escape to from the Dolmabahçe, but differs only in scale for the architect, Nikoğos Balyan, was responsible for both. Its half-dozen rooms are furnished with the full measure of 19th-century opulence: gilt, Persian carpets, Russian candlesticks, Bohemian crystal, more gilt and painted panels of Bosphorus scenes.
Open: 09.00–16.00hrs. *Closed:* Monday and Thursday. Admission charge.

Tea shop – Turkish style

◆
LALELI CAMII

Ordu Caddesi, Eminönü
This, the Tulip Mosque, is best known for its showy subterranean market surrounding a small fountain, packed with bargain clothes shops and called the 'Laleli Vakiflar Çarşısı'.
The complex was built for Sultan Mustafa III (1757–1774) by Mehmet Tahir Ağa and the stone-built prayer hall is one of the finest baroque buildings in Istanbul. Of the many eloquent period details the finest are its exaggerated cornices, engaged columns and the octagonal drum pierced by windows alternating with half apses. The interior of the prayer hall is richly inlaid with

coloured marble, but is often closed for structural repairs. To the west, in a dark, street-level enclosure, stands an octagonal mausoleum which contains the tombs of Mustafa III and Selim III.

◆
MAHMUT PAŞA CAMII
Vezirhani Caddesi, Eminönü
This delightful and original octagonal mausoleum is tucked behind the mosque of the same name. Both were built in the late 15th century for Mahmut Paşa, a Byzantine nobleman who converted to Islam after the conquest, but it seems to be more in the Moorish than the Ottoman decorative tradition. Its marble exterior is inlaid with zellig mosaic – cut ceramic tiles of blue, black, turquoise and green which create geometrical swirls of stars. There is nothing else quite like it in the city.

◆◆
MAHMUT PAŞA HAMAMI
About 275 yards (250m) downhill from the mosque (above), Mahmut Paşa Hamamı Sokaği, Eminönü
Originally twice the size when it opened in 1476, the magnificent carved plasterwork in the three domed chambers of this *hamam* (bath house) is currently being restored.

MARCIAN'S COLUMN see **KIZTASI**

◆◆
MESIH MEHMET PAŞA CAMII
Aksemseddin Caddesi, Fatih
This beautiful and original mosque, built on a terrace overlooking a small park, was constructed in 1585 for Mesih Mehmet, the eunuch governor of Egypt who was infamous for his cruelty. He is buried in the small arcaded courtyard shaded by cypress trees. The portico hides two lodging rooms which look both into the domed prayer hall and out over the park. The interior of the mosque is dominated by a delicately carved marble mihrab arch, bordered by elegant Iznik tiles.
Open: hours of prayer.

◆◆
MEVLEVI TEKKE
Galip Dede Caddesi, Beyoğlu
The monastery of the Mevlevi brotherhood, better known as the Whirling Dervishes, was built in 1491 and led the city's musical and poetic life until it was closed in the 1920s. It is now a museum and is a delightful, tranquil place off one of Beyoğlu's more characterful streets, itself named after a celebrated 17th-century Mevlevi poet. The *tekke* comprises a courtyard surrounded by sheikhs' tombs, an overgrown cemetery, kiosks, a terraced garden and an 18th-century octagonal lodge which houses the wooden dancing floor for the brotherhood. The rooms in the upper gallery exhibit the musical instruments, costumes and distinctive hats of the different branches of the Mevlevi. It also displays an elegant collection of original manuscripts and illuminated volumes of Turkish court poetry, the Divan Edibiyati.
Open: 09.30–17.00hrs. *Closed:* Monday.

◆◆
MIHRIMAH CAMII
Fevzi Paşa Caddesi, Fatih
The single dome and minaret of the Mihrimah Mosque rise majestically beside the land walls and the Edirne gate. The mosque is built on the summit of the city's sixth hill and celebrates Mihrimah, the favourite daughter of Süleyman the Magnificent. It was built in the 1560s by Sinan and is one of his most innovative structures, a model for dozens of baroque and rococo structures built later. The dome is supported by four great side arches linked by the attenuated towers of corner buttresses. This allows the high but non-load-bearing walls to be pierced with windows. The internal effect is magnificent, a soaring hall flooded with light. So as not to disturb this quality the marble side galleries are placed in flanking chambers. The portico entrance to the mosque faces the domed arcade of a *medrese* to create an enclosed fountain courtyard.
Open: hours of prayer.

MILITARY MUSEUM see **ASKERI MÜZESI**

◆◆
MISIR ÇARŞISI (EGYPTIAN SPICE BAZAAR)
Yeni Camii Caddesi, Eminönü
Within this celebrated L-shaped covered bazaar you can buy Iranian caviare, gold, spices, ceramics and roasted nuts. It was built in the 17th century as part of the complex that surrounded Yeni Mosque. The rents from the long row of shops went to a trust that maintained the mosque buildings, a charitable school and a hospital. It got its 'Egyptian' tag indirectly, for the trust also received, as a gift from the sultan, all the import duties from Egyptian goods that came into Istanbul.
Open: 09.30–18.00hrs. *Closed:* Sunday.

The 88 vaulted rooms of the Spice Bazaar contain a huge array of spices and other goods

◆◆

MOZAIK MÜZESI (MOSAIC MUSEUM)

Torun Sokaği, Eminönü

The Imperial palace of the Byzantine emperors occupied the whole area south of the Hippodrome to the sea. It had been something of a ruin for centuries before the Turkish conquest and the remaining traces were swept away during the building of the Blue Mosque.

In the 1930s, excavations revealed one surviving portion: a magnificent mosaic of animals, hunting and fighting which once covered 203 square yards (170sq m) of pavement beneath a colonnade. In its original position it is now sheltered in the Mosaic Museum and contention still reigns over its date. Opinions range from the 4th to the early 6th century AD.

Open: 09.00–17.00hrs. *Closed:* Tuesday. Admission charge. Photography charge.

◆

MURAT PAŞA CAMII

Between Millet and Adnan Menderes (Vatan) Caddesi, Fatih

This stern, strong mosque perfectly expresses the spirit of the age in which it was built, some 16 years after the Turkish conquest of Istanbul. It was commissioned by Murat Paşa, one of the Mehmet the Conqueror's most trusted generals and a Muslim convert from the last Imperial family of Byzantium. Though built in the Greek tradition, with alternating brick and stone courses, it follows the tradition of Ottoman architecture already established at Bursa with geometric precision. The building has a simple dignity and was easy to reproduce elsewhere in the Ottoman provinces, but at the heart of the Empire in Istanbul it was soon bettered by the classical architects of the 16th century.

Open: hours of prayer.

MUSEUM OF TURKISH AND ISLAMIC ART see **TÜRK ISLAM ESERLERI MÜZESI**

◆◆

NIŞANCI MEHMET PAŞA CAMII

Fatih Nişanca Caddesi, off Yavuz Selim Caddesi, Fatih

Mehmet Paşa, Nişanci (Keeper of the Seal) to Murat III, built this delicate, classical mosque in the 1580s. It is approached through an elegant garden courtyard, an arcade of ogive arches round a fountain.

A large central dome, supported on eight high apses, covers the square prayer hall. Finely carved columns extrude from the limestone wall, framing each apse in an arch. Their capitals fade into the elaborate *muqarna* (cascades of stalactites) cornice, while the squinches alternate with scallops and arches.

Open: hours of prayer.

◆

NURU OSMANIYE CAMII (THE SACRED LIGHT OF OSMAN)

Nuru Osmaniye Caddesi, Eminönü

The terraced precinct of the Nuru Osmaniye Mosque is one of the main routes to the

Covered Bazaar. Built in the mid-18th century, it is the first of Istanbul's many baroque mosques and was commissioned by Mahmut I but completed and named by his brother, Osman III.
The mosque consists of a single high dome above a square prayer hall, supported by over-large, wheel-like arches. Inside, the effect is far better, for the unbuttressed walls are pierced with numerous windows. Above the gallery is a fine carved wooden calligraphic frieze, gilded to flicker in the twilight gloom of a line of oil lamps.
Open: early to dusk.

◆
NUSRETIYE CAMII
Necatibey Caddesi, Beyoğlu
Built by Sultan Mahmut II to celebrate his destruction of the mutinous Janissary Corps on 14 June 1826, the mosque is aligned perfectly with the Selimiye barracks of his new army across the Bosphorus.
The mosque was designed by one of the Balyan family, and is an early example of the downward slide of Istanbul's baroque mosques into excessive ornamentation, with camouflaged buttresses, an ormolu minbar top and marble and gilt window frames inside.
Open: hours of prayer.

◆◆
ORTAKÖY
European shore of lower Bosphorus (Boğaziçi)
The tree-lined shore at Ortaköy is particularly animated for the Sunday street market and in the evenings. The shore-front is packed with cafés and the

The dramatic mosque at Ortaköy

narrow streets behind are lined with bars, small restaurants, craft and junk shops. The baroque mosque on the shore, Ortaköy Camii was built for Sultan Abdül Mecit I in 1854 by the architect of the Dolmabahçe, Nikoğos Balyan. It is one of his most successful creations. A pair of tapering minarets flanks the soaring dome of the prayer hall which, since 1973, has been framed by the first Bosphorus suspension bridge. It looks even better at night when a chandelier glows faintly out through the windows of the mosque like a spiritual beacon to passing boats.

◆

RAMAZAN EFENDI CAMII

55 yards (50m) east of Kuvayi Milliye Caddesi, Fatih

This neighbourhood mosque with its unpromising exterior and dank modern porch conceals an exquisite small rectangular prayer hall entirely riveted with Iznik tiles. The narrower red border tiles that frame the windows are particularly rare examples. The mosque also boasts an elegant minaret and a marble washing fountain. It is attributed to the great architect Sinan, who would have been 95 when it was finished in 1586.

Open: hours of prayer.

◆

ROXELANA HAMAMI

Ayasofya Meydani, Sultanahmet, Eminönü

The Ministry of Culture has established a permanent display of Turkish handwoven carpets in these opulent marble baths, named after the powerful wife of Süleyman the Magnificent. It is an ideal chance to inspect a Turkish bath without having one. Designed by Sinan and finished in 1556, these baths consist of two identical sets of rooms for men and women. The domed entrance hall, known as the *camekan*, is magnificently furnished with a central fountain, coloured glass, elaborate cornices and a brilliant blue on white frieze. Here customers would hire a booth to change and rest afterwards, or sit gossiping at the café. The second, three-domed hall was known as the *soğukluk*. It was moderately hot and often housed the lavatories and, as here, a raised marble platform for initial scrubbing. The third chamber, the hot room, is known as the *hararet* and always contains a central heated massage platform, the *gobek tasi*. Here it is an elegant hexagon inlaid with coloured marbles. Washing was performed at the fountains and basins round the walls, or separate rooms could be rented out for family groups.

Open: 10.00–17.00hrs. *Closed:* Sunday.

◆◆

RUMELI HISARI

European shore of Bosphorus (Boğaziçi)

This majestic medieval castle overlooking the Bosphorus at its narrowest point is all the

more astonishing for being built in less than four months. Its sea gate is defended by an outer barbican and by the tall sea tower, while the castle's two other large towers look inland from either side of a steep valley. The curtain wall joins these and two smaller towers to form an irregular enclosure. Inside there is an open-air stage above the stump of a minaret, all that remains of the fortress's mosque. The rest of the interior has been planted as a park, with benches amidst the cannons and capitals.

Rumeli Hisarı played a decisive part in the Ottoman conquest of Constantinople under Mehmet the Conqueror. In 1451, Mehmet demanded a piece of land opposite the existing castle of Anadolu Hisarı from the Byzantine Emperor, who by this time, surrounded by Turks, was unable to refuse. By overseeing the building himself, hiring 3,000 workers and assigning each of the main towers to his three chief viziers, Saruca Paşa, Halil Paşa and Zaganos Paşa, Mehmet completed the fort between April and August 1452. His cannons were then trained on ships supplying the city with wheat from the Black Sea. An example was made of one defiant Venetian boat which was sunk and its crew members impaled. Cutting off the food supply contributed considerably to the success of the siege in the following year. Since then the fort has been used as a garrison and prison; it was restored in 1953 to mark

Rumeli Hisarı – medieval guardian of the Bosphorus

the 500th anniversary of the Conquest of Constantinople. Summer concerts are held here, as well as performances from the Istanbul Festival.
Open: 09.30–17.00hrs. *Closed:* Monday.

◆◆◆
RÜSTEM PAŞA CAMII

Ragip Gümüspala Caddesi, Eminönü
This striking mosque was built by Sinan for Süleyman the Magnificent's Grand Vizier and son-in-law, Rüstem Paşa, in 1561. Its chief glory is the magnificent Iznik tiles with which it is covered inside and out, though the mosque's position itself is unique. It sits on a massive rectangular substructure containing shops whose rent once paid for its upkeep, and is approached up a dark staircase in the corner. Once on the mosque's terrace, notice the curious double porch with its second low roof resting on a row of columns. You cannot miss the tiles which grace the front wall. The tomato-red colour dates them to the finest period of Iznik production (about 1555–1620). Inside, most of the prayer hall is decorated with floral and geometric tiles, leaving only a few rounded surfaces to stencils. The dome sits on four semidomes and four arches which span four octagonal pillars. There are galleries, supported by pillars, on both sides of the mosque and if they are open you should climb up to admire the tile design which decorates their walls.
Open: hours of prayer.

◆◆◆
SADBERK HANIM MÜZESI

550 yards (500m) south of Sarıyer Vapur Iskelesi (pier), upper Bosphorus (Boğaziçi)
This astonishing collection of Ottoman ethnographic and archaeological exhibits is housed in a magnificent late 19th-century *yalı* (mansion). The house was built by an Armenian politician and diplomat, Manuk Azaryan Efendim, who died in 1922. The museum was founded by Sadberk Koç, the now-deceased widow of one of Turkey's leading businessmen, Vehbi Koç, and opened in 1981. The museum is divided into two sections. To the right as you enter is an excellent museum shop and the exhibition of Ottoman ceramics and clothing. To the left, in a palatial black marble space, the history of the Anatolian civilisation from the Neolithic era to Byzantium is told by objects uncovered by archaeologists, accompanied by informative explanations.
The Ottoman wing on the first floor contains the best display of fine Ottoman ceramics, from the world-renowned centres of Iznik and Kütahya, to be found anywhere in Istanbul.
The second floor is mostly devoted to turn-of-the-century costumes. Everything from underclothes to shoes, often made of sumptuous silk and velvet, is embroidered with gold thread. This dazzling display of opulence gives some impression of the richness of 19th-century Istanbul.
On the other side of the museum are the archaeological exhibits.

The first floor is devoted to Anatolian prehistory.
It begins with a striking 7,500-year-old mother goddess figure, an extremely early example of a figurative religious sculpture, and goes on to show examples of writing introduced to Anatolia by the Assyrians from Mesopotamia.
This geometric cuneiform alphabet was incised on wet clay tablets which were then baked to keep a permanent record of edicts, decrees and contracts.
Later artefacts on the half-landing and next floor include Hellenistic gold diadems of oak and olive leaves so fine they would rustle in the lightest breeze, and a delightful small collection of individual terracotta full-length female figures, known as *tanagras*.
The top floor holds objects from the time of Jesus to early Byzantium, showing the sculptural development from distinctly pagan and sexy torsos of the gods to Christian crucifixes.
Open: 10.30–17.00hrs. *Closed:* Wednesday.

ST JOHN OF STUDION see **IMRAHOR CAMII**

ST MARY OF THE MONGOLS see **KANLI KILISE**

SS SERGIUS AND BACCHUS CHURCH see **KÜÇÜK AYASOFYA CAMII**

ST STEPHEN OF THE BULGARS see **BULGAR KILISE**

Selling pigeon food – and attracting a crowd

♦♦♦

ŞEHZADE CAMII (THE PRINCE'S MOSQUE)

Şeyzadebaşı Caddesi, Eminönü

This magnificent mosque and mausoleum was built to commemorate Prince Mehmet, the beloved eldest son of Süleyman the Magnificent. It was the first major building entrusted to Sinan in the 1540s and has a light decorative touch that is missing from his later works. Unfortunately the complex is closed for restoration, but when it re-opens the magnificent tiled tombs of Prince Mehmet, Ibrahim Paşa and Rüstem Paşa should not be missed.

SELIMIYE BARRACKS see **HAREM FERIBOT ISKELE**

◆◆◆
SOKULLU MEHMET PAŞA CAMII

Şehit Mehmet Paşa Yokusu, Eminönü

This is a gem amongst Istanbul's small mosques for its jewel-like Iznik tiling and elegant proportions. It was built in 1571 for the wife of the eponymous Mehmet Paşa, then Grand Vizier under Selim II, by the masterful architect Sinan.

The main entrance to the mosque is up a flight of stairs, beneath the massive gateway, which gives an entrancing first view up over the undulating domes of the complex. The soft ogive-arched portico and solid gatehouse still function as a *medrese*, providing a sonorous background for visitors in the rhythmic murmur of young boys reciting the Koran. A hint of the splendour to come is given by the elegant blue and white faience inscriptions above the windows in the seven-domed porch.

Passing time under the dramatic faience inscriptions on Sokullu Mehmet Paşa Mosque

The interior is dominated by the far wall, ornamented with a breathtaking and bold series of Iznik tiled panels. Koranic inscriptions are surrounded by dizzy, spiralling floral patterns and borders. The second and third levels of the wall are covered with a particularly elaborate and fine tulip design. The *minbar* (the thin pulpit from the stairs of which the Friday sermon is delivered) is entirely covered in Iznik tiles and is the only one of its kind in the city. Apart from the Iznik lunettes above each window the rest of the building is dressed with a finely carved pale, almost white, stone. This lends a sense of tranquillity and strength to contrast with the vibrant decoration.

The balcony is supported by dignified polychrome arches on slender marble columns. Beneath it, to the right of the entrance, the original ceiling of arabesque panelled and painted wood can be seen. Embedded in the *minbar* and the mosque walls are four pieces of dark green stone, reputably fragments of the *ka'ba*, the holy stone at the centre of Mecca.

Open: hours of prayer.

SPICE BAZAAR see **MISIR ÇARŞISI**

Looking over the Golden Horn to the Süleymaniye Mosque

◆◆◆
SÜLEYMANIYE CAMII ✓

Süleymaniye Caddesi, Eminönü
The Süleymaniye Mosque is the grandest, most magnificent piece of Ottoman architecture in Istanbul. It was built by Sinan between 1550 and 1557 and is the heady culmination of his lifelong service as architect to Süleyman the Magnificent.

The Mosque

As in all great mosques, this prayer hall is preceded by a courtyard. A rich collection of antique columns, capped with stalactite capitals and a lozenge frieze, support the domed arcade. The external western gate (which contains the apartment of the mosque's astrologer) and the west door of the mosque are both prominently embellished and higher than the arcade, adding a processional grandeur but introducing ungainly corner columns, from which the arches span at different heights. The central fountain, with its frieze of acanthus leaves, was just a decorative feature as ritual washing is performed in covered arcades between the buttresses of the prayer hall. Four minarets of different heights rise from the corners of the courtyard. The four are said to signify Süleyman's position as the fourth Ottoman ruler of Istanbul, their 10 balconies his position 10th in line from Osman, the founder of the dynasty.
The prayer hall is the most serene and awesome in Istanbul. It is constructed from pale stone, so finely dressed that mortar was required only as a lubricant. Minimal decoration and scrupulous masonry has created a harmonious interior with an almost sculpted quality. This is especially apparent in the massive piers, enhanced by strong cornices and deep carved mihrab niches at ground level. Coloured stone,

either red or black, is used only to stress the spans of the high supporting arches. The mihrab arch is encased in Iznik tiles and surrounded by jewel-like bursts of light that flicker from the high eastern wall.

Sinan reworked the plan of Ayasofya with its three aisles to create this single hall, but structurally they are very similar. Four piers, aided by great columns, carry the arches that support the central dome. A pair of opposing semidomes assist and are themselves supported by a hierarchy of lesser domes. The potentially ugly external buttresses are hidden beneath steep ribbed domes and corniced aviaries, or used to create shadowy washing galleries.

Precincts

In the packed cemetery behind the mosque stand the octagonal colonnaded tomb of Süleyman and the smaller mausoleum of his wife Roxelana, known here by her Turkish name, Haseki Hürrem. Both tombs are covered in some delightful Iznik tiles but are often closed. The views north over the city and the surrounding school buildings are panoramic, and give a good impression of the encircling network of lesser courtyards. Amongst them are the mosque hamam, caravanserai, public kitchen, lunatic asylum, medical college, primary school and two pairs of *medrese* for the four orthodox schools of law. Sinan's modest tomb is to be found at the northern corner of the square.

Open: daylight hours.

◆◆◆

SULTANAHMET CAMII ✓ (BLUE MOSQUE)

Eminönü

The exterior of the Blue Mosque, opposite Ayasofya, is the last word in classical order and harmony. It is impossible to be unmoved by its romantic silhouette: a mountainous cascade of leaded domes rippling groundwards while six minarets pierce the sky. At night these are illuminated and seagulls weave amongst the carved limestone.

The mosque was built for Sultan Ahmet I by Mehmet Ağa, a pupil of Sinan, and was inaugurated in 1616, just seven years after the work began. Until the court moved from the Topkapı Palace in the mid-19th century, it was the favourite destination for the sultan's ceremonial procession to Friday prayers. It retained a prestigious position well into the 20th century, when 16 muezzin made the call to prayer, one for each minaret balcony.

The mosque courtyard is immense and serene, entirely enclosed by a covered arcade supported by antique columns. The small central fountain is entirely decorative, as washing before prayers takes place in covered arcades along the northern and southern walls.

The vast interior is wonderfully rich, flooded with fields of colour and light as the morning sun passes across the windows of the east wall. The square

Slender, fluted minarets signal the splendid exterior of the Blue Mosque

prayer hall is roofed by an array of domes and semidomes, increasing in size as they rise to meet and buttress the central dome. The four central piers, which in other similar buildings are fully integrated into the load-bearing dynamic of the building, have been fluted here and are known derisively as 'elephant feet'. They squat cumbersomely in the open space and with the inadequate restoration work on the stencilled decoration rather spoil the overall effect.
Iznik tiles in the side galleries and the mihrab are marvellous. They mark the culmination of the ceramic tradition of Iznik, and according to popular lore the production of such a quantity exhausted the last master potters and began the decline in Iznik ware.

Precincts: Cavalry Market, Kilim and Rug Museum
The Cavalry Market is an elegant shopping street lined with up-market souvenir shops and carpet dealers, just below the mosque to the east. The ramp which gave entrance to the sultan's lodge now houses a fine kilim collection and there are also rugs and carpets displayed in the vaults below the east wall.
Kilim Museum open 09.00–16.00hrs; *closed* Sunday and Monday. *Rug Museum open* 09.30–17.30hrs; *closed* Saturday and Sunday. Both collections often close out of season.

Carpet repairs in Cavalry Market

Carpets and Kilims
Think of the word 'Turkey' and 'carpet' is never far behind. However, evidence at the site of a 6000BC Anatolian shrine to the mother goddess suggests that the weaving of kilims is much the older craft. The oldest known carpet, from central Asia, is a mere 2,500 years old.
The difference between a carpet and a kilim lies in the way they are made. A carpet is made up of thousands of short pieces of thread, knotted on to a backing of parallel threads and trimmed to equal lengths. In Turkey these are usually decorated on the Persian pattern, like a stylised garden or a traditional prayer mat, with its arch design.
Kilims were produced by Turkey's nomadic tribes from roughly spun wool, locally dyed. They are woven, have no pile and are usually geometric in design, though there is a Balkan floral tradition as well.

◆

SULTANAHMET TÜRBESI (TOMB)

Hippodrome, Eminönü

Osman II built this tomb in 1620 for his father Ahmet I. It is a square chamber with eight hanging arches that support a dome decorated with a lively zigzag motif. The lower walls are covered with good but late Iznik tiles. Behind the sultan's tomb, which is surrounded by those of princes and Murad IV, are four cabinets filled with mother-of-pearl reliquaries, Koran stands, silver candlesticks and brass calligraphic stamps for cauterising wounds.

Open: 09.30–16.40hrs. *Closed:* Monday and Tuesday.

◆

SULTAN MAHMUT II TÜRBESI (TOMB)

Divan Yolu Caddesi, Eminönü

The octagonal chamber housing the sultan's tomb was built in 1838. It is a piece of pure French Empire style, a fitting tribute to this great Westernising monarch who reigned from 1808 to 1839. Its marble vaulted dome, Koranic frieze and glittering chandelier look down on a cluster of velvet covered tombs, for Mahmut was later joined by many of his descendants.

Open: 09.30–16.30hrs. *Closed:* Monday and Tuesday.

◆

TAKSIM AND THE MUNICIPAL ART GALLERY

Beyoğlu

The traffic-filled avenues that radiate from Taksim Square are the heart of modern Istanbul. The square is not pretty, surrounded by a number of hideous high-rise blocks and dissected by a tangle of roads. On its east side is the modern, ill-fated opera house which has twice burnt down. The Independence monument in the western corner was created by Canonica, an Italian sculptor, in 1928 and celebrates Atatürk and other founding fathers modelling the Turkish Republic out of the Ottoman Empire. North of the square along Cumhuriyet Caddesi, the Municipal Art Gallery is a modern grey gallery housing a good collection of Istanbul landscapes and genre scenes painted by Turkey's foremost artists.

Open: 10.00–17.30hrs.

◆◆

TEKFUR SARAYI (PALACE OF THE SOVEREIGN)

Hoca Çakir Caddesi, Fatih

Tekfur Sarayı is a majestic, Byzantine three-storey ruin. The floors, roof, courtyard and balconies have long gone, leaving an attractive façade with two rows of polychrome window arches separated by a delicate frieze of brick and marble. Clamber up one side on the land walls and appreciate the dramatic view that was enjoyed from the seven windows of the top storey. Built around 1300 on the perimeter wall of the Blachernae Imperial Palace, after the conquest it housed the sultan's menagerie and was later converted to industrial use before becoming a ruin.

Open: daylight hours.

◆◆◆
THEODOSIAN WALLS ✓

These great land walls, built to protect the Byzantine capital, extend four miles (6.5km) from the Sea of Marmara to the Golden Horn. Some areas are broken and overgrown, but the undulating masonry is essentially intact and rivals Piranesi's etchings in its romantic decay. Certain stretches have been recently and thoroughly restored. Energetic tourists will want to walk the whole of the path, taking the squatters' huts, rubbish, dead ends and busy dissecting roads in their stride. Others might prefer a taxi ride beside the walls, with judicious breaks at some of the gates (*kapısı*), Tekfur Sarayı and the five-sided fortress, Yedikule (see separate entry).
Within a hundred years of its foundation in the early 4th century, Constantine the Great's city had outgrown its original walls. A new line was built just over a mile (2km) further west but they fell in an earthquake in AD447, the same year an attack was expected from Attila the Hun. Motivated by this horrifying threat, the citizens were marshalled under the four rival horse-racing factions and each allotted a section of the wall to build. A contemporary inscription boasts: 'By the command of the Emperor Theodosius II, the prefect Constantine erected these strong walls in less than two months. Scarcely could Pallas Athene herself have built so strong a citadel in so short a span.'

For a thousand years these walls remained the last word in defensive fortifications. The first line of defence was a wide moat, flooded from internal reservoirs. This moat was bordered by a low parapet, itself overlooked by a 30-foot (9m) outer wall studded with 96 towers. In turn this was overawed by the main wall, 40 feet (12m) high and 16 feet (5m) thick, which was punctuated with another 96 towers alternating with those of the outer wall. A system of military gates and internal terraces allowed for the rapid reinforcement of any sector. There were five arched gateways, each equipped with a drawbridge, that allowed the civilian population to move in and out of the city.

Walking the Walls

The strategic junction of the land and Marmara sea walls was reinforced by a distinctive Marble Tower, now a feature of the coastal park. It served as both a Byzantine state prison and a seaside pavilion for the emperors. The Byzantine military gate just the other side of Avenue Kennedy is known as the Gate of Christ.
The first civilian gate was Yedikulekapı, just north of the great, seven-towered castle. The Golden Gate within it was reserved for ceremonial occasions. The wall north of here is the most attractive section, flanked on either side by vegetable gardens and cemeteries. The length round Belgradkapı has been completely restored. The gate

The Theodosian Walls, which guarded the city for 1,000 years

was renamed when Süleyman the Magnificent captured the great Serbian citadel and settled its artisans in this area. Half a mile (1km) further, Silvirikapı was known as The Gate of the Life Giving Spring by the Byzantines, after the spring in the Monastery of Zooduchus Pege, 550 yards (500m) west through Seyit Nizam cemetery. Just east of the gate is the Mosque of Ibrahim Paşa which was built in the mid-16th century by Sinan and is currently being restored. A rather squalid succession of ruined towers leads on to the restored Mevlânakapı which was named after the famous Whirling Dervish brotherhood. The walls then improve and you have to run the gauntlet of the traffic on Millet Caddesi before reaching the Topkapı (Cannon Gate) with its 1453 memorial. It was known in Byzantium as the St Romanus Gate but was renamed after the conquest to commemorate 'urban', the super-gun of its day which was sited in a battery just to the west. Within the gate are taxis and cafés servicing the giant bus and coach station just beyond the walls. About 220 yards (200m) due east of the gate is the elegant Sultanahmet Camii (see separate entry). The next section received the brunt of the Turkish bombardment and the ruined walls gradually recover their stature as you climb towards Edirnekapı, the Adrianople Gate. At 253 feet (77m) above sea level, it is the highest point of the walls and is the gate through which Mehmet the Conqueror rode stirrupless into the captured city on 29 May 1453 on a white horse. Just within the gate rises one of the city's most prominent mosques, Mihrimah Camii; some 550 yards (500m) later you reach the elegant façade of Tekfur Sarayı (see separate entries). It was through a corner breach just south of this palace that the Janissaries first broke into the city.

The rest of the walls are not Theodosian but date from the 12th century when the whole area was remodelled to make room for Blachernae Palace, which stretched from Tekfur Sarayı to the Golden Horn. The Egri (crooked) Gate then served as the palace back door but now lets on to the cemetery round the 18th-century tomb of Hazret Hafiz, a Companion of the Prophet. From here the walls drop down to join a surviving fragment of the sea wall that once stretched all along the Golden Horn.

TOPHANE see **KILIÇ ALI PAŞA CAMII**

The Library of Ahmet III, centre-piece of Topkapı's Third Courtyard

◆◆◆
TOPKAPI SARAYI ✓

Babihumayun Caddesi, behind Ayasofya, Eminönü

The Imperial Gate (Bab-ı Humayun) is at the northeast corner of Ayasofya, by the Fountain of Ahmed III. This original palace entrance leads into the first courtyard, now a car-park, where tickets are sold.

The Topkapı is a vast and rambling palace, the residence of the Ottoman sultans for 400 years. It is not only an incomparable museum but the finest surviving example of secular Ottoman architecture in Istanbul. It occupies the site of Byzance, the Greek town first established in the 7th century BC. In the palace's heyday its walls enclosed an enormous park that stretched south to the

Sea of Marmara and north to the Golden Horn. The name Topkapı means Cannon Gate, from a portal in the sea wall which bristled with artillery. The palace was conceived and laid out by Mehmet the Conqueror in the 1460s as a place of government. It remained so until 1541 when the old residential palace, on the site of the university, burnt down. Süleyman the Magnificent, under the influence of his wife Roxelana, then moved the harem to the Topkapı. It proved to be a disastrous decision, allowing the passions of family life to become inextricably linked with affairs of state. The harem as we see it today was built piecemeal during the reigns of Murat III (1574–95), Mehmet IV (1648–87) and Osman III (1754–57). At its height, the palace had some 5,000 inhabitants – slaves, cooks, government officials, apprentices and students as well as the sultans and their families and concubines. Improvements and additions continued until 1855 when Abdül Mecit moved into the Dolmabahçe Palace.

The Courtyard of the Divan

Each courtyard in the palace was more private than the last. The outer courtyard contained bakeries, hospitals, porters' and carriers' quarters and the Imperial mint. The next courtyard, through Orta Kapı, the middle gate, was reserved for government business. Known as the Courtyard of the Divan, it was laid out by Mehmet as a serene wooded space with five pathways radiating between trickling fountains and grazing gazelles. Even on government days (four times a week), when the court might contain over 5,000 people, visitors remarked on the unnatural silence of the place. The entrance to the harem is down the left-hand path, where you will have to queue for tickets for the half-hour tour (see below). Near by, beneath the same wide portico, are the domed rooms of the *Divan*, or ruling council. Both of these rooms were redecorated during the reign of Ahmet III in the rococo style, but in 1945 one was restored to its late 16th-century Ottoman decoration. The Inner Treasury beyond houses the palace collection of weapons and armour, mostly fine Turkish pieces, including Mehmet the Conqueror's sword. The courtyard's right-hand path leads past a huge Byzantine capital through the courtyard wall to the old palace kitchens and storerooms. Here the great palace collection of Chinese and Japanese ceramics is displayed, along with lesser exhibits of European porcelain, Ottoman kitchen utensils, glass and silver. The Chinese porcelain, said to be the third best collection in the world, was amassed by Süleyman the Magnificent. It begins with 13th-century celadon ware and proceeds through the porcelain of the 14th to 17th centuries. Metal spouts and bands are Turkish additions though the Chinese also had a canny ability to cater for foreign tastes, as the 18th-century Chinese

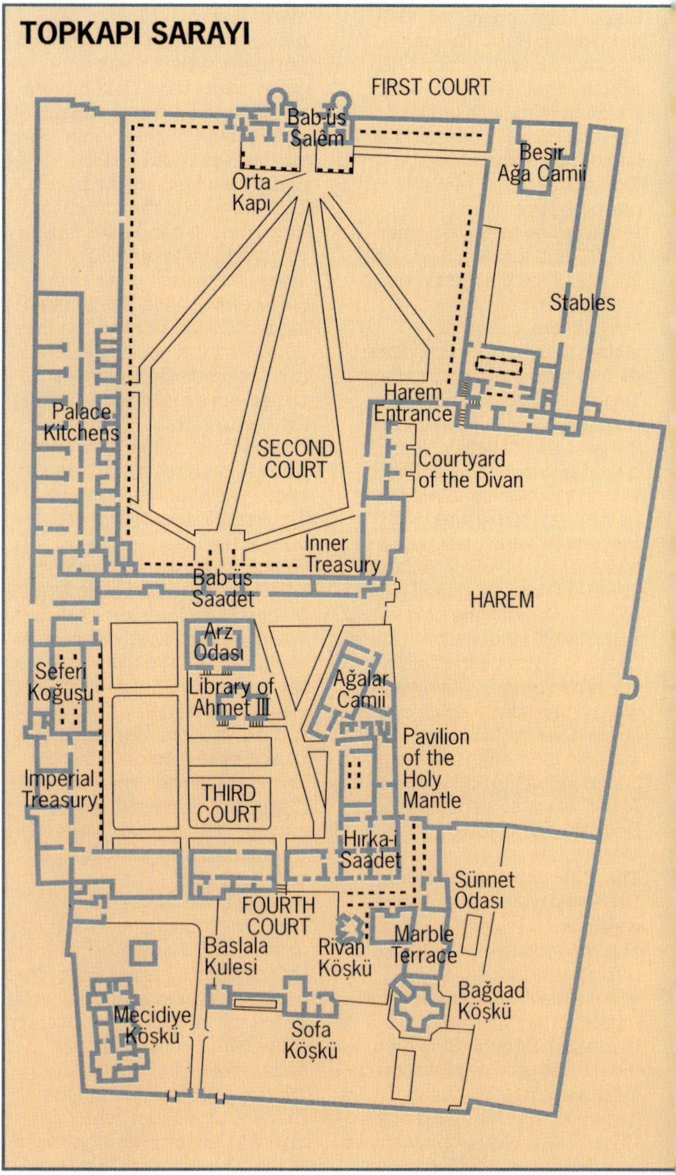
TOPKAPI SARAYI
FIRST COURT
Bab-üs Salêm
Besir Ağa Camii
Orta Kapı
Stables
Palace Kitchens
Harem Entrance
SECOND COURT
Courtyard of the Divan
Inner Treasury
Bab-üs Saadet
HAREM
Arz Odası
Seferi Koğuşu
Library of Ahmet III
Ağalar Camii
Pavilion of the Holy Mantle
Imperial Treasury
THIRD COURT
Hırka-i Saadet
Sünnet Odası
FOURTH COURT
Baslala Kulesi
Rivan Köşkü
Marble Terrace
Bağdad Köşkü
Mecidiye Köşkü
Sofa Köşkü

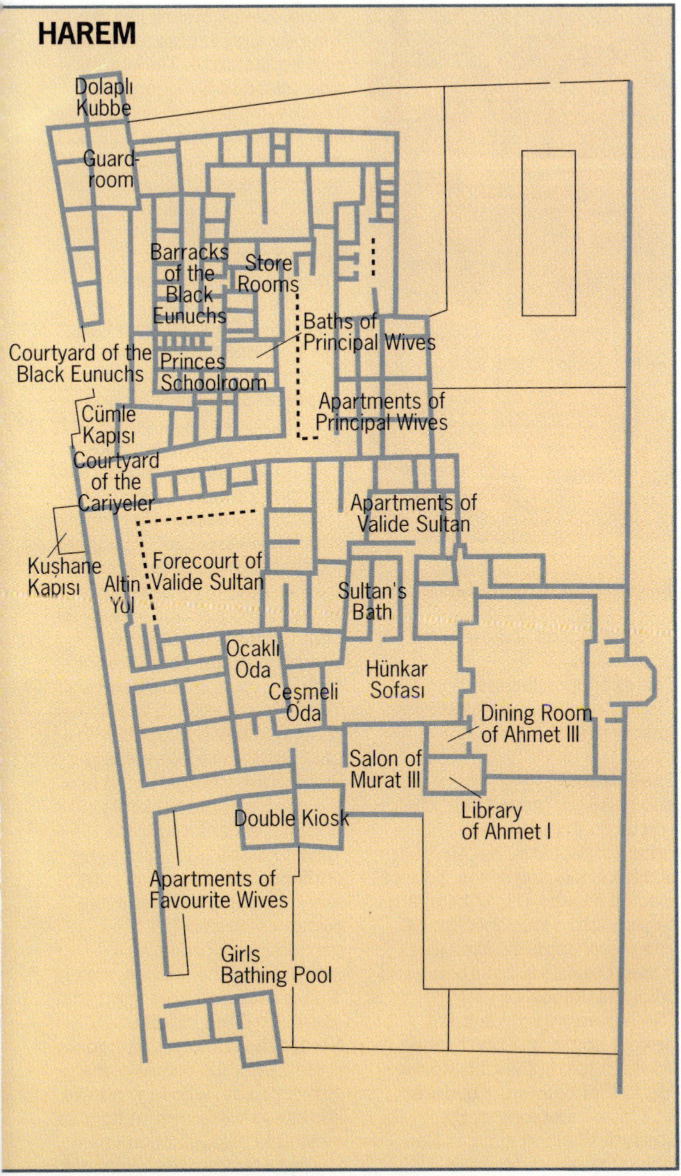
HAREM
Dolaplı Kubbe
Guard-room
Barracks of the Black Eunuchs
Store Rooms
Baths of Principal Wives
Courtyard of the Black Eunuchs
Princes Schoolroom
Apartments of Principal Wives
Cümle Kapısı
Courtyard of the Cariyeler
Apartments of Valide Sultan
Kuşhane Kapısı
Altin Yol
Forecourt of Valide Sultan
Sultan's Bath
Ocaklı Oda
Hünkar Sofası
Çeşmeli Oda
Dining Room of Ahmet III
Salon of Murat III
Library of Ahmet I
Double Kiosk
Apartments of Favourite Wives
Girls Bathing Pool

Sumptuous detail in Topkapı Palace

'Delft' wall tiles and calligraphic plates testify.
The exhibition finishes with a display of elaborate Japanese Imari ware.

The Harem

The half-hour guided tour whisks you through many of the principal rooms in this labyrinth of interconnecting suites. You are ejected into the Third Courtyard reeling with a kaleidoscope of images: of exquisite Iznik tiles, gilded fireplaces, bathrooms and colourful domes.
The harem was the sultan's private home, a series of suites in which his mother, his wives (up to four of them), children and his concubines were housed. Walking into it is like falling into an underwater world, for the first rooms are entirely tiled in blue, turquoise and aquamarine. The entrance was guarded by a corps of black eunuchs who acted as go-betweens with the outside world into which the sultan's women were not allowed. The eunuchs lived in tiled dormitories off the first, pebble-floored corridor.
The first suite of rooms was occupied by the valide sultan, the sultan's mother, who was the supreme figure in the harem. Her dining room, with its peacock feather tiles and gilded palanquin, is particularly fine, and several of her rooms contain magnificent wholly-tiled chimney-pieces.
Next come the sultan's rooms which are surprisingly intimate for such a great sovereign. The marble bathroom has heavy gilded baroque taps and a vast central bath, into which water would have run down the fish-scale cascade on the back wall.
The Hall of Padishah is a domed reception hall equipped with a gallery for musical evenings.
Beyond the salon of Murat III is the glorious corner library of Ahmet I, with magnificent views, natural light, niches for additional oil lamps and rare emerald-coloured tiles in the corners of the roof. A connecting door allows a glimpse into the famous, small dining room, entirely lined with charming floral still-lifes.
Next to the sultan's sitting room is the Cage, the rooms of the crown prince, whose windows and doors were secure against inevitable assassination attempts by younger claimants

or their mothers. They are adorned with the highest quality Iznik tiles and the domed ceilings are lined with stamped, gilded and painted leather.

The Third Courtyard

The third gate is known as the Gate of Felicity (Bab-üs Saadet) and leads into a courtyard of more intimate layout and dimension. Most of the buildings round the edge of the courtyard, now offices, were part of the palace school which trained all the future administrators of the Ottoman state. Just beyond the gate is the Throne Room, Arz Odası, where the sultan would give royal assent to matters decided in the governing council, the Divan, and also receive foreign ambassadors. Faced in marble, its design dates from the early 16th century but the building needed serious restoration after a fire in 1856. Only the magnificent canopy of the throne and the gilt-bronze chimney-piece survived intact. Behind it, the library of Ahmet III (1719) is an elegant, clean, grey marble building with a double staircase leading up to its gate over a polychrome marble drinking fountain. There are five different exhibitions in the third courtyard. Beginning on the right and continuing anti-clockwise, you can see the Imperial costume collection and the outrageously opulent crown jewels in the Treasury. In the far wall is the world-famous collection of miniatures followed by the palace collection of clocks, and in the far left-hand corner of the court the Pavilion of the Holy Mantle, housing religious relics.

The Imperial Costume Collection

The clothes of the Ottoman sultans and their families have been immaculately preserved, some dating from the time of the conquest in seemingly perfect condition. The earlier costumes, kaftans, coats and slippers, and children's leggings, are mostly silk, often heavily embroidered or edged with fur. A sense of horror creeps in as Western European ideas of fashion begin to impinge in the 19th century, all but destroying this brilliant tradition.

The Imperial Treasury

The second room of the treasury is the emerald room. It displays a glittering collection of the stones, mounted on ornate turban pins, as pendants or necklaces weighed down with cascades of pearls and of course in the handle of the Topkapı Dagger. This extraordinary knife was made as a gift for the Shah of Iran in the mid-18th century, but was brought back to Istanbul when he was assassinated before it reached him. Otherwise the treasury contains gifts from foreign rulers, jewelled armour, Christian holy relics and the magnificent Spoonmakers' 86-carat diamond. Of the four Imperial thrones, one is inlaid with ebony and ivory, another with mother-of-pearl and tortoiseshell, and two are simply made of jewel-encrusted gold!

The Miniatures and Imperial Portraits

Whatever is currently exhibited of the palace's incredible 13,000-strong collection, there will be a number of breathtaking miniatures. Among the most extraordinary are the cycles depicting the shamanistic beliefs and nomadic lifestyle of Turkestan, painted by Mehmed Siyah Qalem, about whom nothing is known. They were found pasted into an album in the palace and date from the 14th and 15th centuries. Of the brightly coloured manuscript miniatures, look out for the recognisable landmarks of the Hippodrome – its obelisk, triple-snake column – and gilded column in the Surname manuscript, commemorating the 52 days of circumcision ceremonies for Prince Mehmet in the late 16th century. The Imperial portraits are imbued with a seemingly inappropriate but charming sensitivity.

The Imperial Clock Collection

This is largely made up of clocks given to the sultans by various European powers. They are fitted with German organs and Austrian mechanisms that used to delight the harem by playing party pieces on the hour.

The Pavilion of the Holy Mantle (Hırka-i Saadet)

This suite of four rooms echoes to continual live Koranic chanting and the trickle of a fountain, which reverberate off the high tiled walls. It contains sacred relics of the Islamic caliphate which were brought to Istanbul after the conquest of Egypt by Selim I in 1519. The collection includes the swords of the first four caliphs and one of the first doors to the *Ka'ba* (holy shrine) in Mecca. The relics of the Prophet include hairs from his beard, a footprint and part of a letter written by him. In the holiest of holies the Imam chants over an ornate case containing the Prophet Mohammed's mantle.

The Fourth Courtyard

Two gaps lead through the far wall into the fourth courtyard, a garden space largely closed to the public. The Konyali Restaurant to the right has a marvellous view up the Bosphorus and out over the Sea of Marmara.

To the left a set of stairs leads up to a terrace and portico surrounding the Pavilion of the Holy Mantle. It contains three ornate tiled pavilions round a pool and commands an unparalleled view up the Golden Horn and of Galata, a view the sultans enjoyed from the Iftariye, the gilded bronze canopy on the edge of the terrace. The first pavilion (köşk) is cruciform, inlaid with marble and tiled, and was built in 1636 by Murat IV to celebrate his victory over Erevan in the Caucasus, hence known as Rivan Köşkü. The most magnificent early Iznik tiles of all adorn the outside of the Sünnet Odası, the rectangular room on the edge of the terrace built for the circumcision of Sultan Ibrahim in 1641 and used for the purpose for the next 200

years. Two vast blue panels on either side of the door, fired in one piece, show intricately decorated animals and birds among fantastic flora, and are amongst the largest panels in Istanbul. The third Bağdat Köşkü was built in 1638 and commemorates the taking of that city the year before. Its tiled interior, inlaid tortoiseshell and mother-of-pearl cupboards and brass fireplace are almost intact and provide a glimpse of the joys of palace life.
Open: 09.00–17.00hrs. *Closed:* Tuesday.

◆◆
TÜRK ISLAM ESERLERI MÜZESI (MUSEUM OF TURKISH AND ISLAMIC ART)

In the Palace of Ibrahim Paşa, Hippodrome, Eminönü
The massive brick and stone palace, built by Ibrahim Paşa in 1523, has been restored and turned into a museum of Turkish and Islamic art. It contains a balance of marvellous pieces and glaring gaps, in particular the barely credible lack of Iznik ware. Ibrahim was a boyhood companion of Süleyman the Magnificent and became his trusted and all-powerful Grand Vizier. He was eventually deposed due to the machinations of Süleyman's wife, Roxelana. Ibrahim was invited to the palace for a cosy tête-à-tête dinner with the sultan and later strangled in his sleep. The first two rooms off the long gallery contain examples of the 13th-century lustreware of the Seljuk Empire. Particularly delightful are the star-shaped

Three Days in a City of 300 Sights
Istanbul grows in interest and complexity the longer you stay. It is said to be dangerous to prolong a holiday beyond two weeks, for fear of never leaving. For those with just three days in hand, the most memorable of the city's sights can be squeezed in. Spend the first day in Sultanahmet, beginning with the **Topkapı Sarayı** and the sarcophagi in the **Arkeoloji Müzesi** (Archaeological Museum), and visiting **Ayasofya** and the **Yerebatan Sarayı** (Basilica Cistern). If the weather is good spend the next day on a trip up the Bosphorus. The third day mixes culture and commerce: the mosaics and frescos of **Kariye Camii**, the towering **Süleymaniye Camii** and shopping in the **Covered Bazaar**.

Museum of Turkish and Islamic Art

tiles depicting hares, leopards, storks and pairs of birds. The succeeding rooms have small collections of ceramics, metalware, bindings, marquetry, glass lamps, miniatures and illuminated calligraphy from the great Islamic civilisations: Mameluke Egypt (1250–1517), the 14th-century Timurid Empire of central Asia and Safavid (1501–1722) and Qajar (1779–1924) Persia.
The great hall of the palace and two smaller adjacent rooms are hung with magnificent carpets, dating from the 13th to the 19th centuries. Notable amongst them are an imitation leopard-skin rug and one bearing the celebrated double tiger-stripe motif.
The basement, its entrance flanked by a furnished black tent, is the real star of the museum. It is devoted to the ethnographic arts and crafts of Turkey's peoples and explains, amongst other things, the traditional methods of dyeing and preparing wool for weaving kilims. It also displays a white felt *yurt*, used by the Turco-Mongolian nomads, the woven black tent of the Semites and Iranians, a stone village hut, and a wooden town house, all fully furnished.
Open: 10.00–12.00hrs, 13.00–17.00hrs. *Closed:* Monday. Admission charge.

◆◆
ÜSKÜDAR
Asian shore of lower Bosphorus (Boğaziçi)
This suburb of Istanbul on the opposite shore is characterised by a calmer and cleaner atmosphere than Beyoğlu and Eminönü. There are no great monuments here, but half a dozen interesting sites within easy walking distance of the central square, Iskele Meydani. The coast road in both directions offers a number of bars and fish restaurants.
The name Üsküdar is a corruption of the Greek name Scutari which was itself derived from Scutarion, a Byzantine palace which stretched along

Üsküdar and the Şemsi Paşa Mosque

the shore here by the Maiden's Tower. There had in fact been an ancient Greek town here since the 7th century BC, known as Chrysopolis, the City of Gold. Whatever the period, Üsküdar was always an important roadhead into Asia. Pilgrim caravans would assemble at Iskele Meydani before making their way east, led by a riderless white camel bearing gifts to the holy city of Mecca from the sultan.

Ayazma Camii
Ressam Ali Riza Bey Caddesi
This wonderful baroque structure was commissioned by Mustafa III (1757–74) in honour of his mother. It was built beside a sacred spring whose water was tapped into a cistern. The architect, Mehmet Tahir Ağa, who also built Laleli Mosque, took full advantage of the sloping position. From the outer courtyard a flight of semicircular steps climbs up to the terrace and the prayer dome rises on arches still higher.

Mihrimah Camii
Iskele Meydani
This mosque with its twin minarets overlooks the ferry landing from a raised terrace. It was built by Sinan in 1548 for Mihrimah, the daughter of Süleyman the Magnificent. Impressive from the shore, the prayer hall is dark and disappointing within. The outbuildings beyond on sharply sloping land are much finer.

Kiz Kulesi (The Maiden's Tower)
Half a mile (1km) south of the ferry pier and 220 yards (200m) offshore rises one of the most famous sites of the Bosphorus, a small island capped by an 18th-century white tower. Despite its romantic looks it has been encrusted by a succession of Roman, Byzantine and Ottoman naval stations. It is associated with one of the most widespread Turkish legends. A king attempted to frustrate a prophecy that his daughter would die from a snake bite. He isolated her from harm on an island. An impassioned passing sailor swam out laden with bouquets and a basket of fresh fruit. He drowned, the basket washed ashore and a serpent, hidden in its foliage, gave the princess a lethal bite. It is also referred to as Leander's Tower though Leander swam to Hero across the Hellespont, not the Bosphorus.

Rumi Mehmet Paşa Camii
Şemsi Paşa Caddesi
Just behind the shoreside mosque, this building looks much like a converted church. The alternating courses of brick and stone, the high cylindrical dome with its undulating line of windows are all typical Byzantine characteristics. In fact it was built after the conquest, but by a Greek convert to Islam, Mehmet Paşa, who served as a vizier to Mehmet II. He used Greek artisans to build the mosque in 1471 and is buried in the octagonal tomb just behind the mosque.

Şemsi Ahmet Paşa Camii
This waterside mosque is one of the most celebrated small mosques in Istanbul. It was built

from purest white limestone by Sinan at the southern end of Iskele Meydani for a vizier of Süleyman the Magnificent. Its position encouraged a pleasingly erratic courtyard .

Yeni Valide Camii
Hakimiyeti Milliye Caddesi
This, the 'New Mosque of the Queen Mother', was built in 1710 by Ahmet III for his mother Gülnus Emetullah. The grey marble courtyard encloses a finely carved fountain shadowed by chestnuts and poplars. Notice the 99 names of God to the left of the mihrab, itself faced with Kütayha tiles.
By the street, the aviary-like tomb, planted with roses, is the most celebrated aspect of the mosque. It is formed from eight ogive arches and wrought iron grills. The valide was also commemorated by a school in the mosque gatehouse and a now crumbling kitchen for the poor just outside.

VALENS' AQUEDUCT see **BOZDOĞAN KEMERI**

◆
VALIDE CAMII
Immediately north of Aksaray Meydani, Fatih
Overawed by flyovers and derided by purists, this late 19th-century mosque is not without its charm. Anyone with affection for the fragile will find the four façades of the prayer hall, decorated with a pasted scrapbook of styles and orders, appealing, especially when dusk catches the crumbling white limestone.
Open: hours of prayer.

◆◆
YAVUZ SELIM CAMII
Yavuz Selim Caddesi, Fatih
Süleyman the Magnificent finished this mosque which had been started by his father, Selim the Grim. It crowns the city's fifth hill, adding a distinctive low dome framed by a pair of minarets to Istanbul's chaotic skyline.
The precincts have a venerable and slightly neglected air. In the enclosed garden to the east of the mosque are three tombs, the octagonal tomb of Selim I, the mausoleum of four of his grandchildren and the 19th-century tomb of his more distant descendant, Abdül Mecit I. The outer courtyard is one of the loveliest in the city. A central fountain is shielded by a 'saracen helmet' dome and flanked by four slender cedar trees. Eighteen polychrome arches all supported by pale grey antique marble columns encircle the intimate space. Each barred window boasts an elegant tiled lunette, fine examples of early Iznik *cuerda seca* technique.
The square prayer hall and its furniture is of an austere and monumental simplicity quite in keeping with the character of Selim I. A single shallow dome, pierced by coloured windows, is supported on rough limestone walls. Two flanking lodging rooms, for students and dervishes, are tacked on to the outer walls. Although it seems generations earlier than the sophisticated Sülemaniye, it was in fact finished only five years before in 1552.
Open: hours of prayer.

From the battlements and towers of Yedikule there are fine views over the city, the Theodosian walls and down to the Sea of Marmara

◆◆◆

YEDIKULE (THE CASTLE OF THE SEVEN TOWERS) AND THE GOLDEN GATE

On the Theodosian land walls, towards the Sea of Marmara (Marmara Denizi)

The ancient state fortress of Yedikule has turned its back on the violent events which have engulfed it for 1,600 years and become a somnolent museum. Its curtain wall now encloses a meadow kept trim by a small flock of sheep. The gatehouse lets in visitors who clamber up stairs to gaze out over the city. To appreciate Yedikule's long history, head straight across the enclosure to reach the Golden Gate (Altin Kapısı), set into the west wall. Though two of the three arches have been filled in it is still easy to identify this as a massive triumphal arch, flanked by even greater marble bastions. It was built in 390 by Theodosius I and originally stood alone on a hill just over a mile (1.5km) outside the city. At dawn and dusk it shone like a beacon as the sun was reflected from the gold-plated gates and gilt statues that crowned the now invisible upper storey. A few decades later Theodosius II included the Golden Gate in the new city walls. He added a protective wall, a smaller outer gate and a drawbridge over the moat so it was still the focus of triumphal processions for the next millenium.

It was Mehmet the Conqueror who added the three round towers to the east and turned the area into a polygonal fortress. Thereafter it served as both a treasury and a state prison. Foreign prisoners lodged in the round tower to

An ancient tradition thrives today

the left of the entrance have left elegantly carved 17th-century graffiti as evidence. The cells within the Golden Gate itself were used for a grim succession of executions, including the first ever murder of a sultan, 18-year-old Osman II. In keeping with the traditional death reserved for the Imperial Osmanli family they managed to 'get the bowstring around his neck whilst the chief of the police crushed his testicles'. *Open:* 09.30–16.30hrs. *Closed*: Monday.

◆◆

YENI CAMII (NEW MOSQUE)

Yeni Camii Caddesi, Eminönü

This monumental cascade of leaded domes by Galata Bridge is a central feature of Istanbul. The most familiar of all the city's great mosques, it is grand but approachable, surrounded by informal trading and swirling flocks of pigeons. In the courtyard, approached through the prayer hall, antique columns support the five polychrome arches of each side enclosing a perfect paved square round a hexagonal fountain. The western door is enhanced by a higher dome and a pair of rare marble columns while the west wall is decorated with a particularly attractive Iznik calligraphic frieze.

The prayer hall is also a perfect square. The gallery along the back and side walls naturally focuses attention on the lighter west wall with its gilded mihrab. The Iznik tiles inside are about a century later than those in the courtyard and much less fine, for the mosque was begun by the mother of one sultan in 1597 and finished by the mother of another nearly 70 years later. *Open:* daylight hours.

◆

YERALTI CAMII

Inland from the blue, harbour master's office on Rihtim Caddesi, Beyoğlu

Walk past the ferry terminal downstream of Galata Bridge for 220 yards (200m), then take two lefts in succession to find the mosque on your right. This underground mosque occupies an old cellar with an ancient history. It originally belonged to a Byzantine coastal fortress which guarded one end of the chain which sealed the Golden Horn from enemy shipping. In the 18th century it was turned into a mosque, after two 7th-century Muslim heroes were 'discovered' in nearby graves. *Open:* hours of prayer.

◆◆◆
YEREBATAN SARAYI ✓ (UNDERGROUND PALACE)

Yerebatan Caddesi, Eminönü

This, the largest surviving Byzantine cistern in Istanbul, is one of the city's most haunting sites. The steep entrance stairway leads into a dimly lit underground forest of pillars, echoing with classical music. A walkway, the music and increasingly dramatic lighting draw you deep into the cistern's

Lights cast eerie shadows in the Yerebatan Sarayı

belly, past illuminated decorated pillars to an area which originally appears to have been some form of ornamental fountain. Here the pillars sit on inscrutable pagan gorgons' heads, symbolically upturned to discharge their power. Despite the tarmac and building above, water still drips melancholically from the ceiling.

Built by Justinian in 532, possibly enlarging on an earlier Constantine cistern, the water originally supplied the Byzantine palace and other buildings on the site of the Topkapı. After the conquest, it was used to water the gardens of the Topkapı Sarayı, but knowledge of the existence of the cistern was mysteriously lost, and it took an inquisitive Frenchman, Petrus Gyllius, to rediscover it in 1545. He was studying the Byzantine remains in the city and had himself let down through a well-head in the basement of a house above after hearing that the locals all got their water, and sometimes fish, by dropping buckets through the floor. In a tiny boat by torchlight he meticulously chronicled the dimensions, 460 feet (140m) long by 230 feet (70m) wide, supported on 336 columns. Over a quarter of the cistern was bricked up in the 19th century and remains so today. The columns, which were quarried from pagan temples, are 26 feet (8m) high, topped mostly with Byzantine Corinthian capitals. Above span remarkable surviving herring-bone brick domes.

Open: 09.00–17.00hrs.

◆◆◆

YILDIZ PARK AND ŞALE KÖŞKÜ

European shore of lower Bosphorus (Boğaziçi), northeast of Beşiktaş

Yıldız was a secretive, walled Imperial palace and is now a public park. The lower entrance gate is beside the Mecidiye Mosque on the Bosphorus coast road. The wooded slopes of the park climb past streams, statues and café kiosks towards the Şale pavilion at the summit.

This palace and park were originally built for the sole use of the reclusive and paranoid Abdül Hamit II. From here he controlled the Ottoman Empire, between 1876 and 1909, through rival armies of spies and police agents. Thousands of trees were planted over wasteland and cemeteries, and a network of secret cellars, telegraph stations and underground tunnels.

Şale Köşkü

Guided tours round this typically ornate, 19th-century palace begin at the left-hand entrance. Painted panels give charming detailed views of the Bosphorus and Yıldız executed by an Italian artist, Zonaro. Also look out for the rosewood chairs which were made by Abdül Hamit himself. More imperious are Atatürk's study, the mother-of-pearl inlaid drawing room and the vast reception room covered in a single 486-square-yard (406sq m) carpet from Henki. The principal staircase is decorated with olive branches flanking a

sunburst incorporating the Ottoman star and crescent. The pacific symbolism was for the benefit of visiting statesmen and monarchs like Kaiser Wilhelm II who were entertained here.
Şale Köşkü open: 9.30–16.00hrs. *Closed:* Monday and Tuesday. Admission charge.
Rest of park open: 08.30–17.30hrs.

◆
ZEYREK CAMII (CHURCH OF THE PANTOCRATOR)

Ibadethane Sokaği, Fatih
This 12th-century Byzantine church once stood at the heart of one of Constantinople's largest monasteries and served as a mausoleum for three centuries of emperors. It was converted into a mosque after the conquest but is now looking sadly neglected. From the eastern approach you can best figure out the curious history of this triple church.
The southern end with the highest dome was built by the saintly Eirene of Hungary, wife of John II Comnenus. After her death the grieving emperor built a smaller chapel to the Merciful Virgin to house her tomb just to the north. The gap between was later filled with another chapel and a shared entrance hall added to the west. A few fragments of the original interior decoration survive: a marble triple door, marble fittings in the apse and some mosaics in the south aisle. If you are appreciative the custodian will lift up the carpet to show you a marble medallion of Samson.
Open: hours of prayer.

EXCURSIONS FROM ISTANBUL

Though the three fascinating towns of Edirne, Iznik and Bursa could be treated as excursions from Istanbul, it is more likely that visitors will want an antidote to the city. All the places below therefore offer a complete change from the pollution, noise and bustle of Istanbul's urban environment.

◆◆
BELGRAD ORMANI (BELGRADE FOREST)

12.5 miles (20km) from Istanbul, above the European shore of the Bosphorus (Boğaziçi) and the Black Sea (Kara Denizi)

Büyükada, the largest of the Princes' Islands

This large expanse of woodland was named after workers from Belgrade were moved here in 1521 by Süleyman the Magnificent to oversee the running of reservoirs, aqueducts and water channels supplying the city. The village of Belgrad, now in ruins, is easily found beside the main road, as are two of the most impressive aqueducts built by Süleyman and his great architect Sinan. Even in Byzantine times water from the two rivers of the area was trapped in reservoirs and channelled in aqueducts to the city, and some of these were used as foundations for the later waterworks. These idyllic and often reclusive sheets of water are still the main attraction and searching for them makes a demanding reason to walk.

◆
KILYOS

European shore of Black Sea (Kara Deniz), 20 miles (32km) from central Istanbul

Take a minibus marked 'Kilyos' from Sarıyer on the European shore of the upper Bosphorus. This is the closest beach resort to Istanbul. It is little more than a village on a great long stretch of sand, though there are a few hotels, restaurants and bars catering for visitors. The surrounding area has good walking, but the medieval Genoese castle above the town is under military occupation. If your excursion lasts more than a day, stay at either the **Turban Kilyos Moteli** (tel: 1-242 0288) or **Kilyos Kale Hotel** (tel: 1-882 1054), both overlooking the sea.

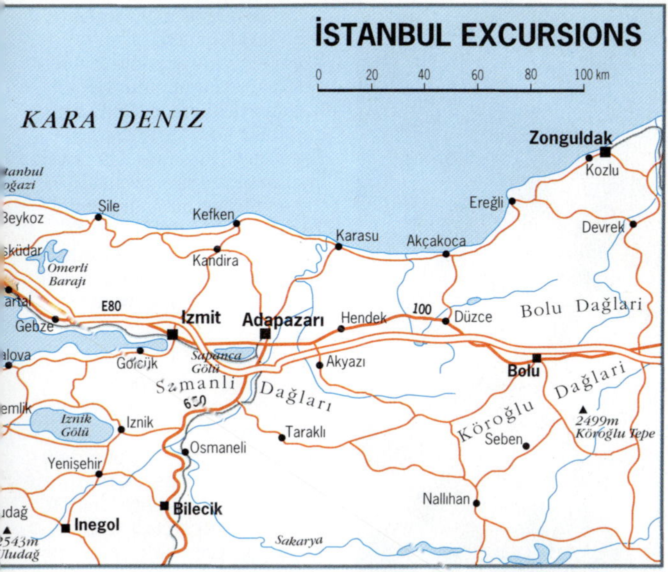

♦♦
KIZIL ADALAR (PRINCES' ISLANDS)

In the Sea of Marmara (Marmara Denizi)

Some 13 ferries make the hour-and-a-half crossing to the largest island Büyükada from Eminönü every day, while faster boats from Kabataş make the crossing in one hour. Until the 19th century the nine Princes' Islands had had a sad history as places of exile and death. On several occasions the wild dogs of Istanbul were rounded up and left to die on Sivri. In 1961 Yassiada served as a prison and law court for the deposed Prime Minister, Adnan Menderes and his associates. They were convicted and hanged here on the night of 16 September. Today however the islands' development as fashionable summer resorts has almost reached saturation point. The largest island Büyükada is the most visited, but both Burgaz and Heybeliada have beaches and restaurants worth sampling. On Büyükada you could stay at the **Hotel Splendid** (tel: 351 6775) and try any of a number of excellent fish restaurants. There are no cars on the island but a plethora of horse-drawn carriages which make round trips through the forested isle, giving intriguing glimpses of magnificent wooden summer homes and isolated sandy coves.

On this map, international distinguishing signs indicate the surrounding countries. Thus: (BG) = Bulgaria (GR) = Greece

A relaxing break from the city

Each of Büyükada's two hills is crowned by monasteries, accessible only on foot. The northern hill houses the deserted Monastery of the Transfiguration in the depths of a pine forest, while on the summit of the southern hill, Yüce Tepe, sits the larger Monastery of St George, a series of dramatic and picturesque buildings.

◆◆
LAKE ABANT
100 miles (161km, 3 hours) east of Istanbul, towards Bolu
This well-known mountain and fishing resort a mile (1.6km) above sea level in the forested Köroğlu Mountains is an excellent rural antidote to the smog of Istanbul. Near by, at Kartalkaya, there is a little skiing on Mount Köroğlu (Köroğlu Tepe) itself in winter. Otherwise the best exercise is walking in the encircling hills. Stay at the **Turban Abant Hotel** (tel: 374-224 5033), which has a sauna and a pool you can jump out of to roll in the snow in winter.

◆◆
ŞILE
Asian shore of the Black Sea (Kara Deniz), 44 miles (71km) from Üsküdar
There are increasing numbers of foreign tour operators offering holidays here, and on summer weekends it is an incredibly popular day out from Istanbul. During the week it is easier to appreciate the decided charms of the bay and harbour, overlooking islands, a black and white lighthouse, a ruined Genoese castle and a long sandy beach.
The **Degirmen Oteli** (tel: 216-711 5048) is a good place to stay.

◆◆
ULUDAĞ
160 miles (257km) south of Istanbul, 11 miles (18km) south of Bursa
If you are in Istanbul but suddenly wish you were in the mountains, Turkey's most popular skiing and mountain resort (December to April) is just a few hours away on the slopes of Mount Uludağ.
Stay in Oteller, the area of the ski resort; the **Kar Otel** (tel: 224-285 2029) is the highest and quietest of the bunch.

Peace and Quiet

Countryside and Wildlife in and around Istanbul by Paul Sterry

Its location makes Istanbul a good base for anyone with an interest in wildlife. Within easy reach of the city there are forests, huge freshwater lakes, attractive coastline and even snow-capped peaks. As an added bonus, vast numbers of migrant birds use Istanbul as a 'flyline' in spring and autumn.

In and Around the City

Among birdwatchers, Istanbul is renowned as one of the best places in the world for observing migrating birds. In particular, birds of prey, storks and pelicans – all large, day-flying migrants – are most visible, and thousands can be seen circling overhead in spring and autumn.

The reasons why Istanbul is such a good spot for migrant birds are partly due to its location and partly to the birds' natural flight patterns. Large birds, such as eagles, storks and pelicans, use rising thermals (columns of hot air) to help keep them airborne. Since land is far better at generating thermals than water, the birds avoid passing over large areas of sea. In order to avoid flying over the Mediterranean and Black Sea on migration to and from their breeding grounds in northern Europe and wintering grounds in Africa, most birds cross at the Bosphorus, where the sea is at its narrowest. Vast numbers funnel through the narrow isthmus of land from March to May and from August to October.

It is generally accepted that the best place to watch migration is on the Camlica Hills, on the Asiatic side of the Bosphorus. Take a ferry to Üsküdar and then a taxi to Büyük Camlica, which is marked by a huge radio mast. This is the best spot in autumn. The lower hill of Küçük Camlica is generally better in spring. Arrive in the early morning in order to catch the first wave of migrants as the air begins to warm up.

Although the migration of large, soaring birds is undoubtedly the city's wildlife highlight, there are other opportunities for observation even if your holiday is entirely city-based. During the summer months, swifts and alpine swifts scream overhead, recognised by their slender, swept-back wings. The alpine swift is the larger of the two. Unlike its plain, dark brown relative, it has a distinctive white throat and belly separated by a black collar. Black kites are ever-present scavengers of rubbish and are recognised by their obvious deeply forked tails. Palm doves are also frequently seen throughout the city, feeding on the ground in small groups.

A pleasant change from the bustle of Istanbul is to take a boat trip along the Bosphorus or to the Princes' Islands in the Sea of Marmara. Ferries leave Eminönü at Galata Bridge regularly; birds that can be seen include several species of gull. Also look out for shearwaters, flying, or rather gliding, on stiffly held wings. They are dark above but pale underneath, the contrast becoming evident when they bank from one side to another.

White stork in flight

White Stork

If you travel anywhere away from the city, to smaller villages and towns, you are likely to see white storks. These large and stately birds, with black-and-white plumage and long, red bills, nest on rooftops, and are sometimes encouraged to do so by the owners placing cartwheels there. Storks feed on frogs, reptiles and insects and prefer wetlands and fields in which to forage. They are summer visitors to Turkey, spending the winter months in Africa. In migration, many hundreds of thousands pass through the country on their journey to other parts of Europe. March and April are the best months in the spring (when the birds are flying north), while August and September are best in autumn for the return passage.

Lake Iznik

To the south of the Sea of Marmara, on the Asiatic side of the Bosphorus, lie three large freshwater lakes that are excellent for wildlife. Lake Iznik is the closest to Istanbul, lying about 100 miles (160km) from the city. Take the road to Izmit and then on to Yalova. From there, head south to Orhangazi, where a road heads east to the town of Iznik and passes close to the northern shores of the lake for much of the way. Stop at suitable vantage points and scan the open water and reed-beds for such birds as white storks, egrets, herons and ducks. The waterside vegetation is good for warblers,

False Apollo butterfly

and watch beside the road for woodchat shrikes perched on posts and wires. These attractive birds, with black, white and chestnut plumage, feed on insects and small lizards which they occasionally impale on thorns in order that they can be dismembered.

Lake Apolyont

Lake Apolyont lies west of Bursa roughly 50 miles (80km) further from Istanbul than Lake Iznik. To reach it, take the road to Bursa which passes through Izmit and Yalova. From Bursa, head west on the road to Bandirma. To view the lake and surrounding vegetation take the road south along the western shores at Uluabet. Vast numbers of waterbirds can be seen here in spring, including pelicans, storks, herons and terns.

Lake Manyas

This is the westernmost of the three large lakes on the southern shores of the Sea of Marmara. It lies roughly 12 miles (20km) to the south of Bandirma. The best and most accessible part of the lake is the northeastern shore, where the Kus Cenneti National Park protects part of the shore and adjacent wetlands. Herons, egrets, spoonbills and pygmy cormorants breed here. To reach the reserve, take the road south from Bandirma to Aksakal and look for signposts after about nine miles (15km).

Mediterranean Flowers

Although influenced by the land mass of Asia, the climate of the coastline around Istanbul is essentially Mediterranean. The summers are long, hot and dry, while the winters are usually relatively mild and wet. In common with other parts of the Mediterranean, many of the plants have their growing period during the winter months and flower in early spring. By early summer many have withered away above ground and survive the summer drought as underground tubers or bulbs. Two flower-rich habitats are characteristic of the Mediterranean where man has cleared the original forests. *Maquis* has colourful and often aromatic shrubs and bushes such as tree heathers, junipers and cistuses while *garigue* occurs on poorer soil and has stunted and often spiny, low-growing species. These two habitats offer the richest hunting grounds for orchid enthusiasts. Members of the bee orchid family are numerous and varied and are an attractive sight in March and April.

Red-rumped swallow

Mount Uludağ

The 8,200-foot (2,500m) summit of Mount Uludağ lies south of Bursa, in Asiatic Turkey, and dominates the countryside for miles around. Bursa is the main access town for the mountain and can be reached from Istanbul by crossing the Bosphorus and taking the road via Izmit and Yalova. From Bursa, a winding road makes its ways to a ski resort, from where excursions on foot can be made to higher elevations. As an alternative, a cable car operates from Bursa and climbs to Sarialan.

As you ascend the mountain you pass through a range of vegetation types. On the lower slopes there are forests of beech with the occasional sweet chestnut and walnut to add variety. At higher elevations, the forests become dominated by firs with an understorey of juniper, finally giving way to open slopes and scree above the tree line. In the spring, meadows are full of colourful flowers including grape hyacinths, crocuses, primroses and orchids. At higher elevations, the same flower species bloom later in the season and thus extend the period in which botanists can enjoy the display.

Birdwatchers will find birds such as firecrests, crossbills and black woodpeckers worth looking for in the forests, and Kruper's nuthatch is a speciality of the area. Above the treeline, look for alpine accentors, shore larks, choughs and alpine choughs. The latter, with their black plumage and curved yellow bills, often become accustomed to man's presence and are on the lookout for discarded scraps of food.

Birds of Town and Garden

Although there are a few species of birds which can tolerate the pollution, crowded streets and lack of greenery that characterise modern Istanbul, the list is rather limited. However, take a tour further afield and you should have more luck. Look for white storks feeding in fields beside the road, while crested larks – small, brown birds with a distinctive crest – are often seen within a few feet of passing traffic. Mature gardens in towns and villages are home to Orphean warblers, nightingales and serins – all good songsters – while swifts and red-rumped swallows feed overhead, catching insects on the wing.

Practical

This section (with the yellow band) includes food, drink, shopping, accommodation, nightlife, tight budget, special events etc.

FOOD AND DRINK

Istanbul's restaurants are many, varied and excellent. The standard of cooking in even the simplest *lokanta* (restaurant) is usually very high, and in the more expensive, licensed restaurants it is often mouth-wateringly subtle. Part of the reason lies in the freshness of the ingredients, both vegetable and animal, and particularly the gleaming silver fish with which the Bosphorus and Black Sea abound. Part of it lies in the well-kept secret that Turkish vegetarian cuisine is one of the most inventive in the world. Innovative cooking has always been encouraged from the top. The kitchens of the Topkapı Palace were an immense cookery school.

Eating Out

From the number of food outlets in Istanbul, you would imagine that the entire population ate out all the time. There is barely a street without a restaurant of some kind and hardly a moment in the day when the cry of hawkers is not audible. The most numerous sell bread rings rolled in sesame seeds, known as *simit*. Other street stalls offer grilled meat, offal and salad filled sandwiches or very thin Middle Eastern pizzas, with a meat topping, known as *lahmacun*. And there are the fish sandwich sellers who cook on moored boats at the Eminönü and Üsküdar ferry terminals and produce the near-irresistible smell of barbecued mackerel. Another street delicacy not to be missed is ice cream (*dondurma*), which is sold from deep refrigerated tubs and regularly stirred to retain its pliable texture. If you want somewhere to shelter or rest your feet for a few minutes there are soup kitchens (*çorbası*) which are most likely to offer *ezo gelin*, a vegetable broth with rice in or *mercimek*, lentil soup. Shops known as *böregi* and *pideci* sell flaky pastry pies (with cheese and meat), known as *börek*, and bread stuffed with cheese, eggs or meat (*pide*). The city is also littered with simple lokantas where up to a dozen hot dishes are kept warm on display and can be chosen by pointing at what takes your fancy. A good filling meal in any of these will be inexpensive, but they are rarely licensed. Other fast food outlets mimic such joints the world over, serving hamburgers and chicken, either barbecued or fried, all with chips and a salad. The majority of Istanbul's licensed restaurants adhere to the traditional Turkish menu explained below. You will eat extremely well for under £10 a head. If you are looking specifically for fish, it is worth checking the menu before sitting down, as some establishments serve only meat dishes. However there are several areas in the city, Kumkapı, Galata and the Bosphorus in particular, where you are guaranteed a memorable marine feast, though the price of an expensive fish like turbot or sea bass will increase the bill. Those with a sweet tooth are catered for in Istanbul's numerous *pastane* (pastry shops), where the puddings divide roughly into two types. A series of milk-based puddings, from *sütlaç* (rice pudding) to *süpangile*, a rich chocolate pudding, contrast with *baklava* and *bülbül yuvası*, pastries stuffed with nuts and steeped in honey.

Turkish Breakfasts

Hotel breakfasts consist of mounds of fresh bread, usually accompanied by jam, cheese, tomatoes, cucumbers and olives. On the streets Turks consume anything from *börek* to *simit* on their way to work.

The Turkish Menu

(See language section for the names of specific dishes.)
A traditional Turkish meal begins with the arrival of a massive tray at your table, laden with different cold hors d'oeuvres known as *soğuk meze*. Famously these include vegetables which have been cooked in olive oil and allowed to cool (*zeytinyağlı*), stuffed vegetables (*dolma*), some seafood and lambs' brains. The waiter will then ask if you want

Ice cream – an Istanbul favourite

any *sıcak meze* (hot hors d'oeuvres), which will be brought as you tuck into the cold ones. Turkish main courses are admirably simple, a piece of fish or meat, often grilled, and served with bread and a salad. Puddings (*tatlı*) or fruit (*mayva*), usually displayed in a refrigerated cabinet, are then offered before a digestive Turkish coffee (*kahve*).

International

There are mercifully few restaurants in this category in Istanbul, since it is often a by-word for inappropriate ingredients, blandly cooked. However, the large chain hotels, the **Sheraton**, the **Hilton**, the **Divan** and the **Çirağan**, all have good restaurants serving well-prepared international dishes. **Club 29**, Istanbul's trendiest nightclub at weekends, is open throughout the week as a bar and restaurant. At the bottom of Taksim Caddesi, its warehouse casing has been transformed with decorative bravura into a surreal and attractive dining space. Another place popular with journalists and the fashion crowd in Istanbul is **Taksim Sanat Evi**, Siraselviler Caddesi 69/1, Taksim (tel: 244 2526). It has a marvellous view of the Bosphorus from high up behind Taksim Square and serves an excellent cheese soufflé.
In Eminönü, the garden of the **Yeşil Ev Hotel** serves as a restaurant, with winter tables in its conservatory. It is a convenient place to take a break during sightseeing, for a drink or a snack.

At the beginning of the century, Istanbul was renowned for its Russian restaurants, but there is really only one place to go now for a taste of this neighbouring cuisine. **Rejans**, Olivya Geçidi 15, Istiklâl Caddesi, Beyoğlu (tel: 444 1610) is busiest and most amusing at lunchtime, when local businessmen and diplomats fill its dining room. Stick to the Russian staples like borsch and beef stroganoff which are well prepared, and wash it down with the establishment's own lemon vodka. Not far away in the **Örs Turistik Is Merkezi**, Istiklâl Caddesi 251–3, the Little Italy Restaurant serves Italian food in a calm and quiet environment beneath a wonderful plaster ceiling painted with birds.

Seafood

Though most of the city's better restaurants do serve some fish dishes on their menu, there are places to head for if you want nothing but fish. Kumkapı, which looks on to the Sea of Marmara and the Princes' Islands, is one of the older residential areas of the city, and has long been a hubbub of night-time revelry. From the coastal road, brightly lit Çapariz Sokak leads up to Kumkapı Square, the whole a pedestrian precinct lined with restaurants, tables and displays of fresh fish. You will have an enjoyable meal at almost any of the restaurants, but both the **Beyaz Balina**, Çapariz Sok 32, and **Restaurant Talip**, at no 43 are particularly popular. As you eat, on the street or inside, musicians will serenade you and salesmen offer everything from red roses to plastic dolls. Another popular location for fish restaurants is under the old Galata Bridge; they should move *en masse* to the new bridge which is being built just upstream. Galata Bridge is a vibrantly raffish place, and the food in its restaurants is reasonably priced. The **Olimpiyat II**, at no 22, and the **Duba** at no 80 are particularly recommended.

The best of all the locations for fish restaurants is on the shores of the Bosphorus. By day the bustle of the waterway and the aqueous dancing sun make these waterside restaurants lively and relaxing, and by night the twinkling lights on both sea and land give it a mysterious enchantment.

On the European shore try **Yeni Günes** at Küçükbebek (tel: 263 3823), very popular with locals and correspondingly expensive. Although the **Iskele Gazino Restaurant** just beside the ferry jetty at Yeniköy (tel: 262 8677) has no outside terrace, compensation comes in the form of small ferries which lunge towards you as you dine, apparently about to come through the window and join you at your table. The cold *meze* here are wonderful and if you have not yet had grilled tuna fish, try it.

The fish market at Sarıyer is one of Istanbul's largest and the closest to the Black Sea fishing. After marvelling at the catch, try any of the numerous restaurants around the harbour to satisfy your appetite. They tend to get more expensive as you walk away from the market at Sarıyer, but try **Super Yedigün**, Rumeli Kavağı Iskele Caddesi 29, with its roof terrace in the summer. At Rumeli Kavağı or Anadolu Kavağı – the last stop respectively on the European and Asian shore – there are a dozen or so places to choose from, many of which specialise particularly in vast fleshy Black Sea mussels, sautéed, fried or stuffed.

Turkish

Of the large hotels, the Turkish restaurant at the Divan Hotel, Cumhuriyet Caddesi (tel: 231 4100) is undoubtedly the best, but there are so many good independent restaurants that it is a pity not to try a variety of them.

A number of the best-known establishments, located on either side of the Galata Bridge, are open only at lunchtime and have been serving businessmen for generations. The most spectacular is **Pandeli**, Mısır Çarşısı 1, Eminönü (tel: 527 3909), which hides above the main entrance to the Egyptian Bazaar. Here, in a series of elegant rooms faced with turquoise and white tiles and decorated with a series of simple ceramic pots on a high shelf, you can try the house speciality hors d'oeuvres, a cold platter which includes caviare and other more customary Turkish *meze*, and choose from an excellent selection of fresh fish and grilled meats.

At 60–2 Yalıköşkü Ishanı near the Sirkeci railway station in Eminönü, the highlight of the

Borsa Lokantasi (tel: 527 2350) menu is sea bass stewed in a tomato and onion sauce. Their puddings are also excellent. On the other side of the bridge, and with an even better reputation than either of these is **Liman Lokantasi** (tel: 244 1033). It is right beside the cruise liner docks, which used to be the city's main harbour, and has always been renowned for its fish.

The most lively place to spend the evening in Istanbul is certainly Çiçek Pasaji, halfway down Istiklâl Caddesi from Taksim Square, on the right. This tall narrow alleyway hosts a number of restaurants, all with tables outside and in. Musicians, hawkers and performers move constantly amongst the diners, both Turkish and tourists alike, entertaining and amusing you as you tuck into selected *meze* and kebabs. If you want something a little quieter in the same area, both **Beyoğlu** at Istiklâl Caddesi, Halep Çarşısı 140/17 (tel: 252 3842) and **Haçıbaba Restaurant**, Istiklâl Caddesi 49 (tel: 244 1886) are licensed and have quiet, sheltered terraces.

Back over in Eminönü, just behind Ayasofya one of the underground Byzantine cisterns has been magnificently renovated to house the **Sarnıç Restaurant**, Soğukçeşme Sok (tel: 512 4291). It has a distinctly 'gothic' feel, as you descend into the pillared hall which is set with giant wooden furniture, iron screens and vast candelabra. In winter there is a real fire, and the food,

Tea and coffee are always strong and black

particularly the soup and the boregi, is very good.

Beside the Beşiktaş ferry landing beyond the Dolmabahçe Palace on the Bosphorus, **Hanedan Restaurant** (tel: 260 4854) hides behind a greenery-clad terrace. Here you will find some of Istanbul's best meat dishes, the secret of which seems to be tender ingredients and spicing.

Cheap and Cheerful

If you want a cheap meal but would also like a drink with it (most cheap restaurants are unlicensed) there are two choices. Some of the bars, distinguished by the neon Efes Pilsen advertising, also serve *meze*, though this is not the sort of place for women to go unaccompanied. Otherwise the place to head for is the area around the Yerebatan Cisterns, at the start of the Hippodrome. Both Divan Yolu Caddesi and Yerebatan Caddesi, and Seftali Sokak which runs between them, are lined with restaurants, bars and budget travel agents. **The Pudding Shoppe**, made famous in the first few chilling pages of *Midnight Express*, is at Divan Yolu Caddesi 6, and despite its name is a restaurant with a poor selection of puddings. The **Sultan Pub** at Divan Yolu Caddesi 2 is very popular and conceals a couple of raucous bars behind it. Both the **Vitamin Restaurant** at no 11 and the **Konak Restaurant** at no 66 serve wine with the steaming dishes on display in their windows.

There are a couple of cheap places to use if you find yourself hungry when shopping. **Ulus Lokantsi**, no 78 in the Egyptian Bazaar, is a good cheaper alternative to **Pandeli** and **Havuzlu Lokantasi**, Gazi Çelebi Sok 3 in the Covered Bazaar makes a colourful midday stop.

What and Where to Drink

Istanbul's tap water is perfectly safe to drink, but has a strong chemical taste. In restaurants you will always be offered mineral water (*memba suyu*) or fizzy water (*maden suyu*), and beer or wine. The cheaper establishments will not offer alcohol, though there is no prejudice against it in most of the city's smarter restaurants. Turkish beer (*bira*), either Efes Pilsen or Tuborg, is also on offer in numerous bars. Turkish wine (*şarap*) is very drinkable and comes in white (*beyaz*), red (*kırmızı*) or rosé (*roze*). The safest labels to choose are Villa Doluca and Kavaklıdere both of which are delicious in all colours. Many Turkish diners drink only the local *rakı*, an aniseed-flavoured spirit which turns cloudy in water, though fresh fruit juice is also normally on offer.

There are cafés, largely a male preserve, all over the city which serve strong Turkish tea (*çay*) or coffee (*kahve*) in tiny quantities. Milk in either tea or coffee is unheard of, but sugar is automatically offered on the saucer of a cup of tea.

With Turkish coffee, you should order it either *sade* (without sugar), *az şekerli* (a little sugar), *orta şekerli* (medium sweet) or *şekerli* (sweet). Herbal teas are also popular, though the apple tea you will be offered regularly is usually powdered.

Ayran is a Turkish speciality and very thirst-quenching. It is a watery yoghurt drink with added salt, sold at kebab stalls and börek shops, and is best drunk very cold.

There are a few places worth a detour for a drink. Both the bar at the top of the **Sheraton Hotel** and the one at the top of the **Galata Tower** give excellent views of the layout of the city. But for atmosphere alone the cocktail lounge at the **Pera Palace Hotel** has a unique pre-war feel, enlivened by a magnificent pair of decorative, Iznik, gypsy-ware chimney-pieces as well as excellent cocktails.

A pile of hats

SHOPPING

Istanbul has been a market place, trading on its position between East and West, for 2,700 years. It contains a plethora of shops and markets, many unchanged for hundreds of years, that sell goods for which the city has long been renowned.

Istanbul's most famous shopping landmark is the Covered Bazaar, Kapaliçarşı, a labyrinthine medieval rabbit warren containing over 4,000 shops. Every day of the year, except Sundays and holidays, its brightly-lit alleyways are hung with carpets, clothes, bags and stacked with piles of ceramics, wood and metalwork.

The Egyptian Market (Mısır Çarşısı) by Galata Bridge is smaller but equally enticing. Its wide, T-shaped corridors are lined with spices, nuts and dried fruit in huge sacks.

In addition to these traditional shopping haunts, Istanbul's fashion-conscious society shops over in Beyoğlu and in the city's smarter residential areas beyond and at Galeria, a shopping mall towards the airport. Istiklâl Caddesi, which leads down from Taksim Square, is a pedestrian precinct lined with increasingly up-market shops. North of Taksim Square, shopping continues along Cumhuriyet Caddesi into Nişantaşı.

Antiques

As well as old carpets and occasional Iznik and Kütahya ceramics, Istanbul's antique shops are well stocked with prints, coloured manuscript miniatures and jewellery. One of the city's best shops is **Sofa**, at Nuru Osmaniye Caddesi 42. Here you will find old maps and prints as well as textiles, old and new Kütahya pottery, metal trays, old stone mortars and calligraphy. Çukurcuma Caddesi, behind Galatasaray Lisesi on Istiklâl Caddesi is also scattered with antique shops.

Books
The old books market, Sahaflar Çarşısı, is a small shaded space not far from the Covered Bazaar in Beyazit. As well as beautiful ancient miniatures and prints from old books, it sells art books and textbooks, dictionaries, guide books and a few English novels.

Carpets and Kilims
It is impossible to know where to begin among the thousands of carpets and kilims on sale in Istanbul, but one good rule is not to buy from the first few shops. Not only will this let you see some of the variety on offer, but it might also encourage the salesmen to drop their prices. There are many carpet dealers on Halicilar Sokaği in the Covered Bazaar, among the best being **Adnan Hassan**, at no 90. The carpet shops on Nuru Osmaniye Caddesi are more expensive, with places like **Galerie**, at no 64 and **Aykut**, which has been dealing in carpets for several generations, at no 100. **Kismet**, Nuru Osmaniye Caddesi 84, sells one of the best-made selections of kilim bags and wallets in the city, as well as carpets. Kilims also make amusing shoes as **Şube**, Arasta Çarşısı 131, Sultanahmet have discovered. They sell leather-soled slippers and rubber-soled desert boots made out of carefully chosen pieces of kilim, and are beginning to incorporate the stuff into denim and suede jackets.

Small, silver and delicious

Ceramics
The magnificent techniques and glazes of the 16th- and 17th-century potters of Iznik and Kütahya disappeared in the 18th century never to return. However the tradition of tile making and pottery itself never died, and there are still many workshops supplying the shops of Istanbul with plates, bowls and tiles. **Amphora**, Arasta Çarşısı 147, Sultanahmet, just below the Blue Mosque, sells some of the best of the large-scale hand-made production, direct from the Altin Çini factory in Kütahya. For even finer work go to Sofa (see **Antiques**) or the shop at the **Sadberk Hanim Museum** in Sarıyer up the Bosphorus. They both sell the work of craftsmen and the prices are correspondingly high.

Clothes
Turkish fashion, led by such luminaries as Rifat Ozbek, is going through a confident

phase, as can be seen in the glorious shop windows of **Vakko**, Istiklâl Caddesi 123–5, which sells both men's and women's clothes in cotton, wool and silk. Nesilihan Yarguci is one of the country's leading designers, whose goods can be bought at Kuyulu Bostan Sokak 6 in Nişantaşı and in Galeria. There are a few stores in the Covered Bazaar selling old embroidered Turkish dresses and coats, and a plethora of leather clothing stores (see below).

Leather can be a very good buy

Food
There are two main areas for food buying in the centre of Istanbul – Mısır Çarşısı in Eminönü near the Galata Bridge and the market off Istiklâl Caddesi opposite the Galatasaray Lisesi, Balikpazari. The caviare shop in Mısır Çarşısı sells both Iranian and Russian caviare at a third of London prices and neighbouring shops sell dried fruit and nuts in abundance. Mısır Çarşısı is also the place to stock up on cheap olive oil and pastrami. For specialist imported foods try **Saraylar**, Balikpazari 17 or **Sutte** at Duduodalar Sokaği 21 near by.

Jewellery
If you enter the Covered Bazaar through the Nuru Osmaniye gate, the street ahead of you, Kalpakçılar Caddesi, is a glittering string of jewellers. **Venus**, Kalpakçılar Caddesi 160, sells antique Turkish silver necklaces and strings of translucent amber. **Georges Basoğlu**, at Çevahir Bedesten 36–7 has a good selection of more traditional gold necklaces and gemstone rings. There is a shop beside the Pierre Loti teahouse in Eyüp, which commands a magnificent view down the Golden Horn, where all manner of semi-precious stones set in silver-plated necklaces, rings and bracelets are on sale.

Leather
At their best, Turkish leather clothes are as good as any in the world. For well-designed women's wear the best place is **Derishow**, Akkavak Sok 18A in Nişantaşı or Yeşilcimen Sok 91, Ihlamur Caddesi, Beşiktaş. There are also a host of leather clothes shops in and around the Covered Bazaar. The quality of goods in those on Vezirhani Caddesi outside the market is better, particularly at somewhere like **Angel Leather**. For leather bags and briefcases as well as kilim ones, **De Sa**, Ortakazazcilar Caddesi 8–10 in the Covered Bazaar has a good selection.

ACCOMMODATION

Istanbul's hotels cover the full range from luxurious (five-star) to small unstarred *pansiyons* (pensions), and are conveniently located in three main areas. The smartest international chain hotels are in the New City in and around Taksim and Beşiktaş. In the Old City the Laleli Mosque on Ordu Caddesi sits in the middle of a group of second-class chain hotels and individually owned Istanbul establishments. The area around Ayasofya and the Blue Mosque, Sultanahmet, bristles with cheap *pansiyons* and hostels as well as small hotels in traditional Istanbul wooden houses. These are good value and offer an experience unique to the city.

It is usually easy to find a room in the city, as there appear to be so many, but if you have definite ideas of where you want to stay, booking in advance for mid-summer is a good idea. The prices in the first two categories below vary enormously, as some hotels have been chosen for character and others for their facilities.

Luxury

The **Çirağan Palace Hotel**, Çirağan Caddesi 84, Beşiktaş, (tel: 258 3377; fax: 259 6687), is a new hotel, in the garden of the 19th-century Çirağan Palace, which is itself being converted to house a shopping and conference centre. Right on the shores of the Bosphorus, with a swimming pool which appears to float in the waterway itself, the hotel's interior has been beautifully decorated and the rooms have magnificent views of the water.

The **Yeşil Ev**, Kabasakal Sok 5, Sultanahmet (tel: 517 6785; fax: 517 6780), is the best appointed of the Turkish Touring Club's (TTOK) Ottoman house hotels. It is a pale green, immaculate wooden building, close to Ayasofya, on a quiet side street beside the Roxelana Baths. The rooms, behind lattice wood shutters, are well decorated with brass bedsteads and Turkish carpets, and the calm, tree-shaded, fountain garden behind serves as a restaurant in the summer.

The **Divan Hotel** on Cumhuriyet Caddesi, Taksim (tel: 231 4100) is the most individual of Istanbul's large business hotels. The food in its Turkish restaurant is mouthwatering and with less than a hundred rooms it still has an intimate and personalised feel.

The **Hilton**, Cumhuriyet Caddesi, Harbiye near Taksim, (tel: 231 4646) and the **Sheraton**, Mete Caddesi, Taksim (tel: 231 2121) both have over 400 rooms and all the facilities you would expect of these establishments. The top-floor bar of the Sheraton has the best view of the whole of Istanbul from its terrace.

First Class

The **Hidiv Kasri**, Çubuklu (tel: 331 2651; fax: 322 3436) is an art nouveau villa, built for the last Khedive of Egypt in 1900. Sitting on a hill on the Asian side, above the village of Çubuklu, it commands a magnificent view of the Bosphorus and is set in a delightful wooded garden. The villa has been magnificently converted by TTOK (Turkish Touring and Automobile Club), and is suitable for those seeking a particularly quiet stay in the city. It is not to be recommended for sightseers as it is a long way from the centre of Istanbul.

The **Pera Palas**, Mesrutiyet Caddesi 98–100, Beyoğlu (tel: 251 4560) is the hotel of old Istanbul (even though it is in the New City), where weary travellers off the Orient Express would hurry for their first stationary night. The place still has a great decaying atmosphere, a believable setting for an Agatha Christie murder, but unfortunately a new ring road has recently been built right beside it. Even if you do not stay here, take tea, one of the excellent cocktails in the bar and (tip in hand) take the opportunity to ride up in the old metal lift.

Another TTOK conversion, the **Ayasofya Guesthouse**, Soğukçeşme Sok, Sultanahmet (tel: 513 3660; fax: 513 3669), occupies the entire cobbled street of houses between Ayasofya and the Topkapı Palace. It is a quiet location and unbelievably well situated, and the decoration, though not inspired, is in the 19th-century style of Istanbul. There are also two restaurants in the street and a specialist Istanbul library.

The new **Ramada Hotel**, Ordu Caddesi 226 in Laleli (tel: 513 9300), is a little squeezed in its busy central location, but lives up to the standards of the chain by providing unpretentious accommodation and service.

The **Hotel Sokullu Paşa**, Mehmet Paşa Sok 3, Sultanahmet (tel: 518 1793), is in another converted wooden house, but has the added attraction of its own, albeit small, Turkish bath. The interior has been thoughtfully decorated, right down to the light switches, and the outdoor restaurant, with its marble fountain, is delightful.

Good Value

The **Hotel Alzer**, Atmeydanı 72, Sultanahmet (tel: 516 6262) is

Restaurant at the Yeşil Ev Hotel

right on the Hippodrome with magnificent views straight on to the Blue Mosque. By night, when the mosque is floodlit, the sight is near magical. The rooms are clean and functional, but the traffic can be a bit noisy in the morning.

The modern **Hotel Hali**, Klodfarer Caddesi 20, Çemberlitas, (tel: 516 2170; fax: 516 2172) has the best view of all. From its upper bedroom you can see Ayasofya, the entrance to the Bosphorus, the Blue Mosque, the Sea of Marmara and the Princes' Islands. Unlike the others, this is a well-designed modern hotel with immaculate bath and bedrooms and a good selection of carpets for sale.

Last but not least, the **Hotel Turkoman**, Asmali Çeşme Sok 2, Sultanahmet (tel: 516 2956/7) is tucked behind the Hotel Alzer in a charming old stone house. Breakfast for the 13 rooms is served on the roof terrace but the hotel has no bar or restaurant.

Hotel Ibrahim Paşa, Terzihane Sokak 5, Aldiye Yani, (tel: 518 0394; fax: 518 4457) stands beside the Turkish Art Museum on the Hippodrome with 19 rooms, a roof terrace and a café-bar all recently installed within a traditional Turkish house.

Cheap

The **Optimist Guesthouse**, Atmeydanı 68, Sultanahmet (tel: 516 2398; fax: 516 1928), right next to Hotel Alzer on the Hippodrome, is a shabby but very friendly place. Of the six rooms, the top two have their

Pera and the Orient Express

As the 19th century wore on, the strength of the Ottoman Empire declined. From their embassies in Pera, the old name for the area around Istiklâl Caddesi, ambassadors of the great European powers competed to influence the sultan. The murky worlds of foreign loans, military missions and arms deals mixed in the hushed corridors with the likes of principled reformers, subversive nationalists and the all-pervasive secret police. These bitter realities were masked by a succession of regattas, balls and receptions held in honour of a stream of visiting monarchs.

The reputation that Istanbul gained at this time for diplomatic double-dealing combined with the romantic exoticism of the new Orient Express train to fire European imaginations. Agatha Christie's *Murder on the Orient Express* or Graham Greene's *Stamboul Train* portray this decadent *fin de siècle* atmosphere. The reception rooms of the **Pera Palas Hotel**, built in 1889 specifically for travellers from the Orient Express, or a table at the platform café in **Sirkeci Station**, itself built for the great train, are suitable spots for 19th-century romantics. Another might be **Haydarpaşa Station** on the Asian shore. This soaring coastal edifice was the key link in the great Berlin to Baghdad railway, which in 1895 confirmed the supremacy of German influence in the Empire.

own bathrooms, the others share two. Breakfast is served in the pavement café downstairs, which also serves drinks and snacks throughout the day.

Berk Guesthouse, Kutlugün Sok 1, Sultanahmet (tel: 517 6561), is a tiny family-run place a minute from the entrance to the Topkapı Palace.

NIGHTLIFE AND ENTERTAINMENT

Nightlife in Istanbul is varied enough to suit all tastes, from dance enthusiasts to jazz lovers. Many visitors find that eating *al fresco* in the city offers a whole evening's entertainment in itself. In both Kumkapı and Çiçek Pasaji in Taksim, dinner is accompanied by lively quartets playing traditional music, passing accordionists and hawkers of everything from lottery tickets to red roses.

Bars

Before dining there are a number of venues worth visiting for a drink. Sipping delicious cocktails in the **Pera Palas Hotel** bar, watching the enormous fish in the fish bowl, you could be in a 1930s time warp. Look out for the magnificent gypsy-ware chimney-pieces and take a ride up in the lift before you leave. At the top of the **Galata Tower** there is a restaurant and nightclub from where you can climb out on to the small balcony which encircles the tower. This has a terrifyingly good view and is certainly worth the price of a drink and

Shoe-shine – part of street life

the entrance fee. Some may prefer the Sultan bar at the top of the **Sheraton Hotel**.

Cabarets

There are a number of Istanbul restaurants which put on an evening cabaret show for the diners. These will not be cheap, but floor shows are comprehensive, including oriental belly-dancing and folk-dancing as well as Turkish classical music.

The best known is **Kervansaray**, Cumhuriyet Caddesi 30, between the Divan and Hilton hotels (tel: 247 1630). It is open 19.30 to 24.00hrs and deserves its excellent reputation. If this is fully booked, try **Maksim**, just off Taksim Square, (tel: 244 3134/5869) or **Orient House**, Mithat Paşa Caddesi, Beyazıt (tel: 517 6163), which can be booked through your hotel.

During the summer, your hotel should also be able to arrange a romantic dinner on a restaurant boat, cruising up and down the Bosphorus. If not ring the **Çirağan Palace Hotel** in Beşiktaş and book a place on their boat (tel: 258 3377).

Nightclubs and Discotheques

Istanbul has a good club scene, renowned for the quality of its venues. **Club 29**, is still the place to dance. It also has excellent restaurants at both its summer and winter locations and plays disco to an energetic mixed crowd. In winter you will find it at Nispetiye Caddesi 29, Etiler (tel: 263 5411), in summer on the Asian shore water's edge in the village of Çubuklu (tel: 322 3888).

Also to be found on Nispetiye Caddesi (no 30) in winter is **Samdan Etiler**. A more establishment set-up, the downstairs restaurant is very busy at weekends when reservations are essential. In the summer the place opens as **Samsa**, (tel: 262 1313) on the hills above Yeniköy on the European shore.

Divan in Kuruçeşme on the European shore (tel: 257 7150) is an enormous place. In summer dancing is outside in its dramatically lit garden.

Discorium, Yıldız Posta Caddesi, Gayrettepe, is the place to check for foreign dance bands.

Cinema and Theatre

Istanbul has well over two dozen cinemas, some of which show English-language films with subtitles rather than dubbed. The key words to look for on posters and in your enquiries are '*asil ses*', which means original voice. All the listings can be found in the Friday, weekend section of the *Turkish Daily News*.

Also listed in this paper are the events taking place at the foreign cultural centres and institutes and in Istanbul's main theatre, the **Atatürk Culture Centre** or **AKM** on Taksim Square (tel: 251 1023/5600 ext 254).

Modern Music and Jazz

Finally, if you prefer to while away your evenings in more relaxed and mellow surroundings, there are a number of excellent music bars in the city, mostly found on the European shore of the Bosphorus.

At **Kedi** in Arnavutköy there is an outdoor terrace in use when the weather is right, and the place attracts a wide range of different bands.

Kalem Bar, Cevdetpaşa Caddesi 306/1, Bebek (tel: 265 0448), on the other hand, swings to jazz piano most nights. It is open 12.00–01.00hrs every day.

Less trendy is **Yelkovan**, Muallim Naci Caddesi, Salahanesi Sok 10/2, Ortaköy (tel: 260 5199). Its large top floor space is very informal and while the music varies it is live and laid back most nights. Open from 18.00–02.00hrs daily.

The best jazz-only bar is **Naima**, Arnavutköyderesi Sok 1, Arnavutköy (tel: 263 0578).

WEATHER AND WHEN TO GO

The ideal time to visit Istanbul is in spring, when the parks of the Bosphorus are in blossom; autumn comes a close second. In summer the city gets hot and crowded, and its heavy muggy air seems to trap the pollution firmly at nose level. From late October you should take a thick jersey as there can be short cold spells, and in January and February take an umbrella.

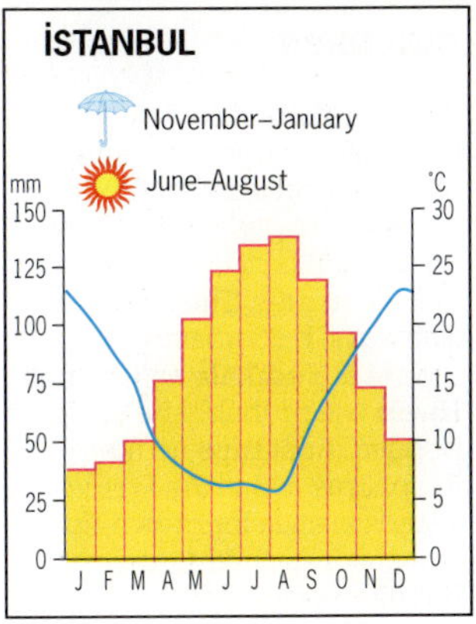

HOW TO BE A LOCAL

Remember that you are in a Muslim country; even in cosmopolitan Istanbul, used as it is to visitors, it would be discourteous not to follow the few simple codes of conduct. Always take your shoes off before entering a mosque, and either leave them outside or take them in and leave them on one of the low shoe racks. Respectful Muslim women cover their heads inside mosques, and this should be imitated by visitors. You might want to wear your own scarf loosely round your neck for such an eventuality. You will also feel more comfortable if you visit holy sites wearing more than shorts and a singlet. At the very least your shoulders and knees should be covered. Be particularly sensitive during Ramazan. At this time it is traditional to fast all day. Even though Istanbul is less strict, it is best to be discreet in your public consumption of food or drink at this time.

Turks are very hospitable and the first greeting is usually an offer to shake hands – this is an important and significant social gesture. You may very well be invited to take tea (*çay*) and it would be impolite to refuse.

Tourists tend to stick together in the nightspots intended for them, so try being a local by finding out what special events are taking place in the city and going along. Buy copies of '*Istanbul: The Guide*' in bookstalls or pick up a free copy in your hotel lobby. The *Turkish Daily News* (in English) also has an entertainment guide in its weekend section with a comprehensive list of theatre, opera, concerts, museums, cinemas and exhibitions. This comes out on Fridays.

To blend in with the locals, male tourists may like to smoke and drink strong black coffee in the cafés; unfortunately, female tourists would stand out here. Smoking is forbidden in cinemas, theatres, city buses and shared taxis.

Finally, bargaining is a way of life – try it; you won't get a bargain but you might just enjoy yourself.

CHILDREN

There is little in Istanbul expressly designed to amuse children, and it is not a good place to bring them until they are beginning to be interested in looking at sites. The numerous stairways, battlements and towers at **Yedikule** and **Rumeli Hisarı** will probably be the most popular. **Boat trips** up the Bosphorus and to the Princes' Islands are fun for grown-ups and children alike. Once on **Büyükada island** you can take a ride in a pony and trap to visit the beach. It is also possible to visit the beaches of the Black Sea from the city, or to picnic in the remarkably unspoiled **Belgrade Forest**. There is a zoo in **Gülhane Park**, beneath the Topkapı Palace but it is certainly a distressing place for adults, and may well be so for today's environment-conscious children.

TIGHT BUDGET

Spending little in Istanbul is very easy, if you can resist the temptation of shopping.

- There are few places in the city that you cannot walk to, and most trips on public transport, whether by boat, minibus, tram or metro cost very little indeed. Even the excursion ticket up the Bosphorus, which will take a whole day, is inexpensive.
- In the **Directory** a couple of campsites and youth hostels are listed which will bring down the cost of your stay.
- You can keep spotlessly clean if your hostel has no hot water by visiting the local *hamam* (baths).
- Even the relatively poor in Istanbul eat out, at the numerous local lokantas , so keeping body and soul together will not bankrupt you either.

FESTIVALS AND EVENTS

March/April
International Film Festival showing Turkish films with English sub-titles as well as foreign films.
June/July
Istanbul Festival of Arts and Culture, which includes international music, classical jazz and rock, and opera, ballet and folk dancing. Tickets are available from the Atatürk Kültür Merkezi in Taksim Square.

SPORT AND LEISURE

There is only one participation sport easily on offer in Istanbul: swimming. There are public pools at the **Burhan Felek Spor Sitesi**, between Kadiköy and Üsküdar, at Tarbaya on the Bosphorus and at Moda Deniz Kulübü, Moda, Kadiköy.
While Istanbul is not a place to come for a sun and sea holiday, it is possible to swim in the Bosphorus, the closer to the Black Sea the better but keep your mouth shut just the same. In summer, swimming off the Princes' Islands is irresistible but crowded.
Football is prominent in Istanbul where some of the country's best teams play. **Inönü Stadium** on Kadırgalar Caddesi below the Hilton in Taksim is a spectacular venue, and even if you do not venture to a game, you will hear victorious supporters insistently hooting car horns after the match.

Directory

This section (with the biscuit-coloured band) contains day-to-day information, including travel, health and documentation.

Contents

Arriving

By Plane

Most visitors arrive at the Atatürk International Airport to the west of the city. From there it is a cheap taxi ride to the hotels in the centre of Istanbul, depending on the route and time of day. All journeys should be metered, so mention it to the driver if he fails to turn it on before you set off.

If you do not want to take a taxi all the way, ask the driver for Ataköy Tren Istasyonu (Ataköy Railway Station) and take an eastbound train into the main Sirkeci station in Eminönü. There are also buses every half hour, from the stop marked 'Havaş' across the car-park at the airport. These take a circuitous route via the domestic terminal and the main Topkapı bus station on the outskirts of the city.

By Train

There are two railway stations in Istanbul. Sirkeci station in Eminönü receives all the European trains, while Haydarpaşa station on the Asian shore at Üsküdar is the terminal for trains from Asian Turkey, Moscow, the Middle and Far East. From Sirkeci, taxis are cheap to the hotels in Beyoğlu, Sultanahmet and Laleli, but from Haydarpaşa you should take a boat from the adjacent jetty to either Karaköy or Eminönü and take a taxi or walk from there.

Bargaining Skills
In theory, bargaining is a discussion between two equals to ensure that seller and buyer are both happy with a price. In practice there is often nothing equal about the contest at all. Tourists unused to the system are embarrassed to dispute the price, nervous of underestimating and looking a fool.
There is one rule for the novice that avoids all this. Unless you are very mean, you are unlikely to underestimate a price in the city. So decide exactly what you are prepared to pay for the object, make a first offer a little below, rise to your price and walk away if you don't get it. Nine times out of 10 you will be called back and the price accepted. Whether the price was the lowest possible is irrelevant, since you yourself decided the price you wished to pay.
As you become more accomplished you can play a more fluid role in this absorbing dialectic, but watch out for the trick of being offered something you do not want as well in exchange for a price rise. Buying two carpets is never cheaper than buying one if you have only got one space on your floor.

Baths see **Hamami**

Camping
With a proliferation of hotels in the city, it is often possible to negotiate bargain rates in some of the cheaper hostels and hotels, but if even these are too high for your purse Istanbul's campsites are all close to the shore of the Sea of Marmara not far from the airport. The best are the **Ataköy Tatil Köyü**, Rauf Orbay Caddesi (tel: 559 6000), or the **Florya Turistik Tesisleri** on Yesilköy Halkali Caddesi, both in Ataköy.

Abstract beauty: tiles in a mosque

Chemists see Health

Crime
Despite the down-at-heel feel of a lot of Istanbul, mugging, bag-snatching and even pick-pocketing are very rare occurrences. This is undoubtedly partly due to the visible police presence, particularly in the tourist areas. Nevertheless, it is sensible not to carry all your valuables and passport with you when you go out.
You would be stupid to try to buy drugs in the city, as most of the salesmen you are likely to meet will also have a close association with the police, who are evidently a tough bunch if you cross them.
All this means that the streets of central Istanbul are safe at almost any time of day and night, though women alone should exercise caution, and remember that a taxi ride from one side of the city to the other will be very cheap.

Customs Regulations
The duty free allowance on entering Turkey is 200 cigarettes and 50 cigars or 200 grams of tobacco (plus an additional 400 cigarettes, 100 cigars and 500 grams of tobacco if purchased from the Turkish duty free shops on arrival); five litres (or seven bottles of 70cc) of alcohol; five bottles of perfume; one camera and up to five rolls of film and 1.5 kilograms of coffee.
Import and export of narcotics is of course severely penalised, as is the export of antiquities.

Disabled Travellers
Pavements and other surfaces in Istanbul are treacherous even for the most able-bodied, and disabled travellers will need determination and a willingness to make frequent use of taxis to make the most of their stay.
Except in the larger hotels there are very few lifts in Istanbul, and even the major museums lack them. Having said that, all of the Topkapı Palace, and most of the city's mosques and churches are accessible to wheelchairs and the people of Istanbul are consistently helpful.

Driving
There is absolutely no need of a car in Istanbul and indeed traffic jams and generally erratic roadsense can make driving dangerous. It can be great fun using the city's prolific public bus, tram, underground and boat system, not to mention the thousands of taxis. If you arrive with a car you might like to park it in one of the city's numerous car-parks and abandon it for the period of your stay.
Drive on the right, giving way to traffic from the right, and beware the local habit of overtaking on the inside. The speed limit is 31mph (50km/h).
When taking your own vehicle to Istanbul, it will be registered in your passport and you must take it with you when you leave the country, unless it has been written off or stolen. In either case, the local police will be able to tell you how to have your passport stamp deleted.
You should also take your

vehicle registration documents with you and an insurance policy. The British Green Card system does not cover Turkey but both the AA and the RAC sell policies which do.
Insurance can also be arranged at the border from the Turkish Touring and Automobile Association (TTOK). If you break down or have an accident, contact the police. TTOK will carry out repairs for you and send you the bill in Swiss francs.
If renting a car you will need to be over 21 and to have held a licence for over a year. International driving permits from the AA are helpful but not essential.

Electricity

Two-pronged round-pin sockets run off 220 volts AC, which means that British equipment needs an adaptor, and US 110 volt appliances will require a transformer as well.

Embassies and Consulates

Since Ankara took over as capital of Turkey in 1922, Istanbul's grand old Embassy buildings have been relegated to consulates.
Australia Tepecik Yolu Üzeri 58, Etiler (tel: 257 7050)
Britain Mesrutiyet Caddesi 26–34, Tepebaşı, Beyoğlu (tel: 252 6436)
Canada Büyükdere Caddesi 107/3, Bengun Han, Gayrettepe (tel: 272 5174)
Ireland Cumhuriyet Caddesi 26A, Elmadağ (tel: 246 6025)
US Mesrutiyet Caddesi 104–8, Tepebaşı, Beyoğlu (tel: 251 3602).

Emergency Telephone Numbers

Police 055 or 666 666
Fire brigade 000
Ambulance 077

Hamami

Turkish baths, known as *hamami*, are a good way to keep clean if you are travelling very cheaply, and a great place for a relax and massage if not. The sexes bathe separately, either in different sections of the baths or at different times. You can choose between a simple sweat in the steam rooms and washing yourself with your own soap and shampoo or an elaborate ritual in which you are washed and massaged by an experienced pair of hands. Try either **Cağaloğlu Hamam** on Hilâli Ahmer Caddesi 34, Cağaloğlu, **Çemberlitas Hamam** on Divan Yolu, Eminönü, or **Çinili Hamam** on Itfaiye Caddesi in Zeyrek.

Health Regulations and Tips

There are no vaccinations required by the Turkish authorities, though it is always advisable to be up-to-date on tetanus, typhoid and polio. As there is no EU health care available in Turkey, you should take out a travel insurance policy, making sure that the policy covers both the European and the Asian sectors.
Mosquitoes may well keep you awake at night, but can be dispersed with local incense coils (spiral tütsü) or plug-in tablet vaporisers. By day, use a roll-on or spray repellent if need be, and it is advisable to bring your own as the local brands may not be as effective.

Tap water in Istanbul is safe though heavily chlorinated, and bottled water is available everywhere. If unlucky, you may catch a bout of diarrhoea and if you have forgotten your own remedy, Turkish chemists (*eczane*) stock them. In every district there is an all-night chemist (*nöbetçi eczane*). They will also treat other minor complaints.

For more serious illnesses turn to one of the international hospitals in the city. The **American Hospital** is at Güzelbahçe Sok 20, Nişantaşı (tel: 231 4050), the **French Pasteur Hospital** is behind the Divan Hotel at Taskisla Caddesi 31, Taksim (tel: 248 4756). The Pasteur Hospital has a good dental clinic, the **Unident Dis Merkezi**.

Holidays

Public

1 January: New Year's Day
23 April: Independence Day; Children's Day
19 May: Atatürk's Commemoration; Youth and Sports Day
29 May: Festival commemorating the capture of Istanbul by Mehmet the Conqueror in 1453
30 August: Victory Day
28–9 October: Republic Day

Religious

The most important of the religious holidays in Turkey are 'Şeker Bayramı', which celebrates the end of a month of fasting known as Ramazan, and 'Kurban Bayramı' which commemorates Abraham's offering of a sheep in place of his son Isaac as a sacrifice.

Traditional military costumes

They both last three days, due to the Islamic lunar calendar but the dates move back 11 days each year in relation to our Gregorian solar calendar. In 1996 they are on 19 February and 30 April respectively. Şeker Bayramı is marked by giving sweets and presents to children and by family celebrations, while Kurban Bayramı sees the ritual slaughter of millions of sheep.

Lost Property

Reports of lost or stolen property should be made to the tourist police at Alemdar Caddesi 6, Sultanahmet (tel: 528 5369). Not much is handed in, but occasionally lost passports do turn up.

Media

It is easy to get hold of foreign-language newspapers and the *International Herald Tribune*, a couple of days old, in both Sultanahmet and Taksim. The English-language *Turkish Daily News* is also on sale in both areas. For entertainment listings look at '*Istanbul: The Guide*' which is available in hotel lobbies and bookstalls. Also look out for '*Cornucopia*' an extraordinarily elegant quarterly magazine devoted to the arts, culture and antiquities of Turkey.

Money Matters

The Turkish Lira's (TL) exchange rate puts thousands of lira into your pocket for every pound sterling. Inflation is very steep, so that the exchange rate is constantly rising. There are 50, 100, 500, 1,000, 2,500 and 5,000 lira coins in circulation, and notes in 5,000, 10,000, 50,000, 100,00, 250,000 and 500,000 (TL) denominations. There are no restrictions on the amount of foreign money you can bring into Turkey, but no more than US$1,000 worth of Turkish Lira may be legally exported. Keep the exchange slips you are given when you buy Turkish Lira so that you can reconvert unused Turkish currency when you leave. The Turkish for exchange bureau is *Kambio*.

Credit Cards

Access, Visa and American Express are accepted in all of Istanbul's smarter hotels, shops and restaurants, but local shops and lokantas will not take them.

Banks

Open Monday to Friday, 08.30–12.00hrs and 13.30–17.00hrs. **Imar Bankası**, on the corner of Divan Yolu Caddesi and Işık Sokaği in Sultanahmet, is also open on Saturday mornings but charges commission. Otherwise banks are closed on Saturday, Sunday and public holidays.

Opening Times

Government Offices 08.30–12.30hrs and 13.30–17.30hrs, closed Saturday and Sunday.

Fishermen on Galata Bridge

Shops 09.30–13.00hrs and 14.00–19.00hrs, closed Sunday. The Covered Bazaar opens earlier, at 08.30hrs (also closed on Sunday).
Museums Istanbul's museums and palaces tend to be closed on either Monday or Thursday, and sometimes both. Use the **What to See** section of this book to check specific sites. Otherwise they usually open from 09.30–17.00 or 17.30hrs. See **Money Matters** for banks.

Personal Safety see **Crime** and **Health**

Pharmacies see **Health**

Places of Worship
Catholic services are held at the Church of Saint-Antoine Istiklâl Caddesi 325, Boyoğlu (tel: 244 0935).
There are working Protestant churches attached to both the Dutch and British consulates, known respectively as the Union Chapel, Istiklâl Caddesi 393, Beyoğlu (tel: 244 5212) and St Helene's Chapel, Mesrutiyet Caddesi 34, Tepebaşı (tel: 244 4228).
Orthodox services take place at Aya Triada, Meselik Sok 11, Taksim (tel: 244 1358) and at the official headquarters of the Greek Orthodox Church, the Patriarchate, which hangs on resiliently in Constantinople. It is at Sadrazam Ali Paşa Caddesi 35, Fener (tel: 521 2532).
Two synagogues still hold Saturday services in the city, Beth Israel, Efe Sok 4, in Şişli (tel: 240 6599) and Neve Shalom, Büyükhendek Caddesi 61, Sishane (tel: 244 1576).

Police
There are tourist police who are responsible for inspecting hotels and restaurants, and ordinary police who deal with crime and traffic. The tourist police, to whom you should report any loss or theft, are at Alemdar Caddesi 6, Sultanahmet (tel: 528 5369).

Post Offices
Post offices are signalled by yellow signs reading 'PTT'. Large ones are open 08.00–20.00hrs Monday to Saturday and 09.00–19.00hrs on Sunday, though the international telephone offices attached are open until 24.00hrs. The main post office is on Yeni Postahane Caddesi, near the station in Sirkeci, but there are other large branches on Istiklâl Caddesi, in Kadiköy, Galatasaray and Usküdar.
Letterboxes are yellow and set in walls, though they can be hard to find.
If you wish to have mail sent to you *poste restante*, make sure it is clearly addressed to you at Büyük PTT, Yeni Postahane Caddesi, Sirkeci, Istanbul.

Public Transport

Boats
These are the most efficient of Istanbul's modes of transport, but necessarily only cover the shores of the city. Piers (*iskele*) in the centre of the city are named after the destination they serve. Buy a metal disc (*jeton*) at the ticket office (*gişe*) by the entrance, and let yourself through the automatic gates. Further out, one pier serves several destinations, but the piers are always manned at the arrival

of boats so you can ask what time your boat goes. Popular destinations are also served by fleets of smaller boats for which you pay the fare on board. Boats leave up to five times a day in summer from Eminönü to make the hour-and-a-half trip up the Bosphorus to Anadolu Kavağı and there are seven high speed ferries a day to the Princes' Islands from Kabataş pier.

Buses
To use Istanbul's big buses buy a supply of tickets from special kiosks or from ticket sellers at central bus stops. The beige minibuses have their destination painted on a board at the front and are particularly useful on the roads beside the Bosphorus. Flag them down as they pass and pay inside. The main city terminals are at Topkapı (tel: 582 1010) and Harem (tel: 333 3763) in Europe and Asia respectively.

An old tram in Taksim Square

Tram
The most recent addition to Istanbul's public transport system is the superb new tramway, a model of its kind. It starts at the Sirkeci station, passes up by the Aya Sofya, Beyazit Meydani on its way towards Laleli. At the Aksaray junction it divides, one line running to the Topkapı bus station by the walls, the other up Vatan Caddesi. The old-looking tram systems in Beyoğlu continues in service. This runs along Istikâl Caddesi in Beyoğlu saving what can become a repetitive uphill walk. Tickets are bought from the ticket office at the top, and from inside the Tünel station at the bottom.

Tünel
This is Istanbul's answer to an underground railway, a piece of track a few hundred metres long which runs from the Karaköy side of the Galata Bridge to the bottom of Istiklâl Caddesi, a particularly steep part of the city. Buy a jeton from the ticket office and let yourself through the automatic gates.

Taxis
These are ubiquitous, cheap and sometimes alarmingly fast. All of the yellow cabs are fitted with meters which should be used at all times.

Dolmuş
Scattered throughout the city (most usefully at Üsküdar and the Eminönü side of Galata Bridge) are ranks of curvaceous 1950s American cars known as dolmus. Despite their incongruousness and the lurking suspicion that they must be driven by gangsters, they

are an Istanbul institution. Used as communal taxis, they ply the fixed route displayed on their windscreens until they are full. Negotiate the price of a seat, hop in and ask the driver to stop where you want. You can always hail a passing dolmus.

Student and Youth Travel
Student status makes no difference to travelling within the city. However, there are a number of hostels you will be able to make use of. Try the **Yücelt Interyouth Hostel**, next door to Ayasofya at Caferia Sok 6/1 (tel: 513 6150/1) or the **Kadırga Student Hostel**, Cömertler Sok 6, Kumkapı (tel: 527 0218).
If you have an ISTC card you will be able to get into cinemas, museums and concert halls at a reduced rate of 50 per cent, but even better, a FIYTO student card should admit you free to museums and sites.

Telephones
Istanbul's telephone boxes do not accept money, so buy jetons from the post office or from booths near a group of telephones. Jetons come in small (*küçük*), medium (*orta*) and large (*büyük*) sizes. If you try making an international call with jetons you will find you have to feed in the big ones at a distracting rate.
International phone calls are better made from a post office (PTT), where there will be either a cardphone with cards on sale, or a metered phone for which you pay the clerk on duty.
To phone Turkey from abroad, dial the international access code followed by 90 (the country code), and then the city code (Istanbul is 212), and number.
From Turkey, international lines are obtainable by dialling 9, waiting for a new tone, dialling another 9 and waiting for another new tone, followed by:

Australia	63
Britain	44
Canada	1
Ireland	353
New Zealand	64
US	1

If you have trouble, the international operator is on 115.

Time
Istanbul is two hours ahead of GMT and seven hours ahead of US Eastern Standard Time. Since Turkey operates daylight saving between late March and late September, only in October is Istanbul a mere hour ahead of London.

Tipping
Most bills automatically include a service charge, but it is usual to leave a little extra on top. Taxi drivers do not expect tips, but if you are feeling generous they love 10 per cent.

Toilets
There are public toilets (*tuvalet*) all over the city, but they are never very clean or enjoyable and they certainly will not have loo paper. What is more they make a small charge.
The city's smarter hotels' plumbing can cope with loo paper, but in most restaurants and small hotels it should be put in the bin beside the loo. This may feel unhygienic at first, but it is far worse for the proprietor if the drains block.

Tourist Offices
The main Istanbul office is at Mesrutiyet Caddesi 56–7,

Beyoğlu (tel: 243 3472). There are also useful and helpful branches in Sultanahmet, at Divan Yolu Caddesi 3 (tel: 522 4903) and at Karaköy Maritime Station, at Karaköy Limanı Yolu Salonu (tel: 249 5776).
There are also Turkish Culture and Information Offices abroad:
Britain First Floor, 170–3 Piccadilly, London W1V 9DD (tel: 0171 734 8681).
US 821 United Nations Plaza, New York, NY 10017 (tel: 212/ 687 2194) and 2010 Massachusetts Avenue NW, Washington DC 20036 (tel: 202/ 833 8411).

Travel Agencies

Most of the useful travel agencies in Istanbul, which can arrange tours of the rest of the country as well as flights and coach tickets for abroad, cluster round the Yerebatan Sarayı (Byzantine Cistern) in Sultanahmet. You can also arrange car hire through them. Among the best are Imperial, Divan Yolu Caddesi 30 and Pacifik, Divan Yolu Caddesi 34.

A comfortable seat in the sun

LANGUAGE

Turkish is a difficult language for visitors to learn and understand, but you will find that many Turkish people speak some German or English. Nevertheless, it is always fun trying out a few basic words, and your efforts will be consistently appreciated by the Turks. Though the alphabet used is similar to the Latin, several letters are pronounced differently, and the addition of various accents further modifies the sounds:

ay = igh as in sight
c = is pronounced j
ç = ch
ğ = the g is silent and a preceding vowel lengthened
i = as in machine
ı = try saying the u in put with a broad smile
j = zh
ö = ur through a rounded mouth
ş = sh
ü = ew through a rounded mouth
y = the y is silent but any preceding vowel lengthened

Basic Words and Phrases

yes	evet
no	hayır
please	lütfen
thank you (very much)	(çok) teşekkür ederim
you're welcome	bır şey değil
hello	merhaba
goodbye	allahısmarladık (said by the one leaving)

goodbye	güle güle (said by the one who remains)
good morning	günaydın
good evening	iyi akşamlar
good night	iyi geceler
how are you?	nasılsınızı
(very) well	(çok) iyiyim
and you?	siz nasılsınızı
I don't understand	anlamıyorum
do you speak English?	ingilizce biliyor musunuz
there isn't any	yok
good/bad	iyi/kötü
big/small	büyük/küçük

Numbers

1	bir	20	yirmi
2	iki	30	otuz
3	üç	40	kırk
4	dört	50	elli
5	beş	60	altmiş
6	altı	70	yetmiş
7	yedi	80	seksen
8	sekiz	90	doksan
9	dokuz	100	yüz
10	on	101	yüz bir
11	on bir	200	iki yüz
		1,000	bin

Travelling and Directions

Where is...?	...nerede?
...the toilet	Tuvaletl.
...the ferry jetty	Iskele...
...the train station	Tren Istasyonu...
...the port	Liman...
left/right	sol/sağ
straight ahead	dümdüz
here/there	burada/orada
How far is...?	Ne kadar uzak?
A ticket for...	...'a bir bilet

Outside the Blue Mosque

return	gidiş-donüş
What time does it leave?	Kaçta kalkiyarı

Time

What time is it?	Saat kaç
What time does it...	Saat Kaçta
...open/close?	açilir/kapalir
soon	yakinda
now/later	simdi/sonra
early/late	erken/geç
Sunday	Pazar
Monday	Pazartesi
Tuesday	Salı
Wednesday	Çarşamba
Thursday	Perşembe
Friday	Cuma
Saturday	Cumartesi
spring	ilkbahar
summer	yaz
autumn	sonbahar
winter	kiş

At Your Hotel

hotel	otel
boarding house	pansiyon
Do you have a room?	Bos odaniz var mıı
single/double	tek/çift
with a double bed	çift kisilik yatakli
hot water	sıcak su
breakfast	kahvaltı
the bill	hesap

Shopping

I want...	...istiyorum
How much is this?	Bu, Kaçadir
cheap/ expensive	ucuz/pahalı
old/new	eski/yeni
beautiful/ ugly	güzel/çirkin
I'll take it	Bunu alacağim

Restaurants and Food

water	su
mineral water	maden suyu
bread	ekmek
fruit juice	meyva suyu
wine	şarap
red/white	kırmızı/beyaz
beer	bira
ice	buz
another	baska bir
menu	yemek listesi
tea	çay
coffee	kahve
milk	süt

Appetizers

patlıcan ezmesi	aubergine paté
piyaz	white beans vinaigrette
çoban salatası	chopped tomato cucumber onion and pepper salad
zeytinyagli fasulye	green beans in tomato sauce
sigara böreği	cheese pie cigars
yaprak dolması	stuffed vine leaves
midye dolması	stuffed mussels
cacık	yoghurt cucumber and herb dip
imam bayıldı	aubergine stuffed with onion and tomato

Main Courses

kuzu	lamb
Pirzola	lamb chops
döner kebab	lamb from spit
şiş kebab	lamb kebab
siğır	beef
şiş köfte	meatballs
bonfile	fillet steak
piliç	chicken
balık	fish
barbunya	red mullet
kalkan	turbot
levrek	seabass
kılıç	swordfish
midye	mussels
karides	shrimp
mercan	bream
palamut	tuna
üskümrü	mackerel

Puddings

baklava	pastry stuffed with nuts and honey
tel kadayif	shredded wheat stuffed with nuts and honey
sütlaç	cold rice pudding
kompostu	stewed fruit
dondurma	ice cream
meyva	fruit

INDEX

Page numbers in *italics* refer to illustrations

Acknowledgements
The Automobile Association would like to thank the following photographers and libraries for their assistance in the preparation of this book.

ANTHONY SOUTER took all the photographs and cover (AA PHOTO LIBRARY) except:
MARY EVANS PICTURE LIBRARY 10 Loutrell Psalter, 13 Abdül-Hamit II
NATURE PHOTOGRAPHERS LTD 96 White Stork (Michael Gore), 97 False Apollo Butterfly (Paul Sterry), 98 Red Rumped Swallow (Kevin Carlson)

Thanks to **Barnaby Rogerson** and **Rose Baring** for their work on this revision